W9-BYO-597

The
Sarbanes-Oxley Guide
For Finance
And
Information Technology
Professionals

Created By

The Sarbanes-Oxley Group
www.SarbanesOxleyGroup.org

Edited By

Sanjay Anand, Chairperson
www.SarbanesOxleyGuide.com

Includes the trademarked SOCKET™ Framework
(Sarbanes-Oxley Compliant Key Enterprise Technology)

Level: Intermediate to Advanced.
Primary Category: Business and Economics.
Secondary Category: Finance and Information Management.

Publisher: Booksurge/CLA Publishing. *Knowledge Fit for a C-FIT-O (Chief Financial, Information, Technology Officer)* ®

DISCLAIMER

ISBN: 1-59457-578-9
LCCN: 20041090033
PRICE: USD $39.95

PRINTED IN THE UNITED STATES OF AMERICA
By Book Surge Printing and Distribution Services, SC

About the Book

(For updates and worksheets, visit www.SarbanesOxleyGuide.com.)

The most comprehensive, authoritative guide to getting your organization Sarbanes-Oxley compliant. Created by the Sarbanes-Oxley Group, this guide provides a foundation and an advanced reference for Finance and Information Technology executives, professionals and consultants who are involved in or are looking to get involved in Sarbanes-Oxley related compliance projects. Amongst other things, the book addresses:

1. Key aspects and components of the Sarbanes-Oxley Act.
2. How to assess if your firm is Sarbanes-Oxley compliant.
3. The road map to compliance including checklists, worksheets and project plans.
4. The business and technology implications and resource requirements for compliance.
5. The future of Sarbanes-Oxley and its impact on corporate America and the world.

The book includes practical, actionable advice that every Finance and IT professional must have at their fingertips as they pursue, or consider pursuing, a journey of Sarbanes-Oxley compliance. Due to the enormity of the Act itself, this book is by no means all-encompassing. Nevertheless, it is the *most* comprehensive guide available and is, without doubt, the most valuable reference book you will need and use for Sarbanes-Oxley in your organization.

About the Editor

(To contact him directly visit www.SanjayAnand.com.)

Fw. Sanjay Anand has 20 years of Information Technology and Business Process Management experience as a strategic advisor, certified consultant, professional speaker and published author. He is the recipient of such industry recognition as the J.D. Edwards Worldwide Consultant of the Year, Northeast Area Special Achievement, Global Enterprise Solutions Outstanding Performance, and Client Services Valuable Teamwork Awards.

Over 100 clients, both large and small, have included companies from a diverse array of industries and geographies, spanning from academia to technology and from Asia to the Americas. He is often referred to as the "Consultant's Consultant" for his training and mentoring skills.

Mr. Anand has been published in such international trade publications as Data Quest, Computers Today, Tech Republic and Information Week, amongst others. His radio presentations have been broadcast to over 120 countries.

He has an M.Sc. in Technology and an MS in Computer Science (*annual gold medal* recipient) from BITS Pilani in India (affiliated to MIT in Cambridge, Massachusetts). He also has an MBA in Operations and Strategy, and an MS in Finance (*summa cum laude* equivalent) from Boston College.

Mr. Anand is the Chairperson of the Sarbanes Oxley Group (www.soxgp.org), and the Executive Vice President at CLA Solutions (www.clasolutions.com).

TABLE OF CONTENTS

PREFACE FOR THE FINANCE PROFESSIONAL

Everyone seems to know what the Sarbanes-Oxley Act entails and that its main objective is to renew investor faith in public companies. There is no doubt that reform of some kind was needed, if only to avoid future economic and corporate fiascoes like the WorldCom and Enron collapses. The difficulty in any reform process is to find a balance between the costs associated with new regulations and the ultimate benefits attributed to the reform. The Sarbanes-Oxley Act has attempted to find this balance by requiring strict adherence to corporate governance practices designed to quickly and accurately report statements of financial position. The ultimate goal of Sarbanes-Oxley is to deliver financial data that is transparent, accurate, timely, and useful for forecasting.

The Board and the CEO said, "Sounds great – sign us up" meaning, "It's the law, now how do we make it happen?" and then they quickly turned the task of managing the compliance effort over to the CFO, who has to get on board and get moving to meet the various deadlines imposed by the Act as set out by the SEC and the PCAOB. The changes required under Sarbanes-Oxley are revolutionary and require visionary leadership and proactive management to ensure compliance. The stereotypical number- crunching CFO is being rapidly replaced by a CFO who must communicate effectively and lead the compliance process authoritatively and diligently. The magnitude of the changes prescribed by Sarbanes-Oxley reaches far beyond the finance department and provides the perfect impetus for organization-wide reevaluation.

Sarbanes-Oxley as a regulatory requirement has broad-reaching implications that will change the way compliance and internal control systems are developed and managed, and as such, it has enormous potential to improve business processes and drive operational and process excellence. Everything from records and information assets management, to corporate communication, to integrating IT will need to be analyzed and optimized in order to meet the compliance and reporting standards demanded by the legislation and investors. As front-runners in this process, finance professionals will be asked to suggest changes and develop systems that meet these demands without undue costs or adverse effects on operational efficiency.

Complying with this legislation is no small task and one that cannot be done in isolation. Although Sarbanes-Oxley is thought of as financial legislation, the reality is that input from across the departments and throughout the corporation will be necessary to successfully implement changes of the size and scope necessary to make Sarbanes-Oxley's philosophy the standard across the board. CFOs will need to get into the operations of the company and understand what drives profits. This fundamental knowledge will help immensely when trying to detect sources of fraud and irregular activity. The close scrutiny of operational practices will undoubtedly lead to improved internal controls, with deficiencies being spotted quicker and major processes (payables, receivables) under continuous review.

While Sarbanes-Oxley covers 11 titled components and consists of 66 sections; section 302, dealing with disclosure controls and procedures, and Section 404, pertaining to internal controls and procedures, are the two sections that are getting the most publicity and will likely pose the greatest challenges. The Certification process identified in Section 302 and implemented by the SEC requires the CEO and CFO to personally certify that the corporate reports they are filing with the SEC are accurate and complete. Section 404 requires the company to disclose the effectiveness of its internal control systems by outlining management's responsibilities for maintaining an adequate control system and assessing the system's performance at the end of each fiscal year. In June of 2003, the SEC, under Sarbanes-Oxley Section 906, required foreign and domestic issuers to certify their financial reports in a separate document with slightly different wording from that under Section 302.

These sections all work in unison to ensure that financial information is reported accurately. The CEO and

CFO must certify the financial reports and the best way to do that is to have inscrutable internal controls. The SEC recommends forming a disclosure committee to oversee the executive certification and control system review process, but any formalized system can be put in place to ensure compliance. The COSO framework for internal controls is another highly recommended best-practices guide for establishing and monitoring a control system and its specifics will be discussed later in this report. Beyond internal controls, compliance with Sarbanes-Oxley will require that information management procedures apply to professional vendors as well.

Professional services providers will be held to a new standard under this legislation and it is imperative that they know what the corporation's policies and procedures are, and that those policies are applied to them as appropriate. Some of the provisions of the Act prohibit professional firms that provide financial services from providing other consultative services like human resource planning, legal services, and business process planning. This is to keep financial information separate and distinct and to mitigate undue influences on the financial systems and data. The standard for penalty is no longer corruption; simply knowing of, or not preventing inaccuracy is enough to bring about sanctions and charges.

The seriousness of Sarbanes-Oxley and the implications of it will be felt throughout the company and it is important to manage the shift in corporate culture as well as the specific processes of compliance. The corporation must adopt as strong a policy of non-tolerance of irregular reporting as it has against sexual harassment or other criminal activity in the workplace. A Code of Ethics will need to be written that includes explicit provisions about the integrity of financial information and if a code is not present, the company will be accountable for why it does not have one. Whistleblowers will also receive protection under Sarbanes-Oxley as the Act mandates that a formal system be put in place to facilitate employees' disclosure of irregular activity and includes a mechanism to sue the company in case of retaliation.

It is extremely important to develop an ethical culture and strong foundation of systems in order to comply with Sarbanes-Oxley. While the government cannot legislate ethics or records management practices it can, and has, imposed significant consequences for noncompliance. The consequences are severe and criminal, with fines of $5 - $20 million and/or 5 to 20 years imprisonment. With stakes as high as these, it is no wonder executives are very concerned about their compliance practices and it is clear that Sarbanes-Oxley is intended to reach far beyond financial reporting and to inspire corporations to adopt systems that are transparent, accurate, and timely.

This Guide will introduce you to the basics of Sarbanes-Oxley and provide some solid frameworks to begin, or build-on, the task of corporate compliance. Some key components of the Act are:

- The Public Company Accounting Oversight Board (PCAOB) was established to monitor company compliance with the act.
- CEOs and CFOs are required to certify all reports before they are filed with the SEC.
- Accounting firms are restricted in the non-auditing services they can provide.
- Audit committees are regulated.
- Code of Ethics or lack thereof, must be disclosed. If there is no Code of Ethics, the company must explain why one has not been adopted.
- Whistleblowers are protected.
- Punishments for securities law violations are now stricter.
- Several real-time disclosures are now mandatory.
- Adjustment corrections, off-balance sheet transactions and pro forma information must be disclosed.
- Officers, directors and owners (of 10 percent or more) are required to report their transactions no later than two business days after the transaction.
- Officers and directors are prohibited from securing personal loans from the company.

- Insider trading during designated blackout periods is limited.
- Both domestic and foreign Public Accounting Firms are required to register with the PCAOB.

PREFACE FOR THE TECHNOLOGY PROFESSIONAL

Aside from the obvious implications of Sarbanes-Oxley on the CFO and the finance department, significant impact will be felt in the Information Technology sector. As CFOs struggle to meet the new regulations, they will seek technology solutions to support an overall financial compliance strategy. Sarbanes-Oxley requires an extremely high level of data security and integrity as well as unprecedented speed of access to financial information. CIOs and CTOs are busy developing and integrating robust tools to support the new financial reporting requirements. Information technology will play a key role in transparent business processes, as it will enable and support the efforts made. As such, IT executives will play a more integral part of financial control in day-to-day operations.

Under the Act, the CEO, CFO, and auditors are required to certify not only the company's financial statements, but also the financial processes. This means that these executives and auditors will need to fully understand the processes underlying the financial data and reporting systems. This will involve significant involvement of the CIO and the technology department. IT is what will ultimately deliver successful compliance so it is necessary for the CIO to play an active and visionary role to fully utilize the current IT system's capabilities and suggest cost-effective upgrades or modifications where necessary. When, in some instances, noncompliance can mean jail time, companies must have reliable and secure computerized systems in place to manage financial data and reporting.

Technology applications that use a consistent data model will provide the foundation for greater transparency, effective decision support, and consistent processes and controls; increasing confidence in external reports and timely access to data. Section 409 requires companies to report changes in financial condition "on a rapid and current basis" and to have systems for "real-time disclosure." The SEC has accelerated filing deadlines for quarterly and annual reports. This will undoubtedly mean an increased need for process integration and rapid access to valid financial information.

The process improvements that are required under Sarbanes-Oxley will enable technology to be used in a way to aid overall business improvement. While often seen as a very expensive cost-center, the strict records management mandated by Sarbanes-Oxley is the perfect opportunity for technology investment that makes sense to even the stingiest CFO. There are a myriad of vendors who are marketing complete Sarbanes-Oxley Compliance Systems and the main job of the CIO will be to determine what combination of software and internal processes will work best – the solution will not likely be from a single supplier but rather a collage of services combined to maximize efficiency at the lowest possible cost. One thing is almost certain; a system of spreadsheet-based planning will be inadequate. Actual spreadsheet error is high enough, but the potential for spreadsheet error is huge. Decision makers are already leery of relying on spreadsheet models, and with the strict consequences imposed by Sarbanes-Oxley, the CEO and CFO will demand a much more structured and secure platform for them to certify the controls are working and the reports are accurate.

The sections of the Act that are most relevant to finance and the CEO are also very important to the IT industry, as it will be expected to provide the practical solutions and pose the most limitations. Charged with analysis and design, systems development and maintenance responsibilities, IT professionals must be cognizant of the following:

- Turning compliance efforts from being just a tactical exercise into true, value-creating strategic IT initiatives.
- Enterprise Resource Planning (ERP) provides a foundation for compliance, performance, and quality.
- Systems based on spreadsheets are insufficient for the demands of Sarbanes-Oxley; procedures must be foolproof, automated, integrated and auditable.

- Compliance systems should have adequate virus and hacker security protection, backup schedules, backup restore testing, and documented disaster recovery plans.
- Business-critical processes should be resident on one platform.
- Real-time information must be accessible in case of problems, from anywhere, at anytime.
- Active enterprise-wide integration of all entities into defined policies, procedures, and processes.
- Application standards in target processes, day-to-day work, problem resolution, system controls, and risk management at all levels throughout the organization.

Part One

Sarbanes-Oxley
For the
Finance Professional

INTRODUCTION

SARBOX SHAKES-UP CORPORATE GOVERNANCE

The Enron fiasco forever changed investor and public reliance on self-regulation measures for accounting and financial reporting. Not since the stock market crash of 1929 and the depression in the 1930's has so much attention been paid to federal securities laws and financial and reporting methodology for public companies. The result has been a staggering shock to the financial and information systems of public companies as executives and their boards scramble to make sense of, and comply with, the new regulations.

The Sarbanes-Oxley Act of 2002 was enacted after the Enron and WorldCom debacles and in response to the resulting dramatic loss of faith in the governance of public companies. As such, this Act significantly affects the day-to-day functions of all top-level management and executives of public companies: particularly the CEO, the CFO and top information officers. The Act creates a five-member Public Company Accounting Oversight Board (PCAOB), which has the authority to set and enforce auditing, attestation, quality control, and ethics (including independence) standards for public companies and gives the PCAOB the right to impose disciplinary and remedial sanctions for violations of the board's rules, securities laws, and professional auditing standards. The SEC has adopted many of the Sarbanes-Oxley provisions and the breadth and depth of these changes ensures that CEOs, CFOs, and CIOs pay close attention to the systems the corporation has set for reporting and auditing of all financial information and securities transactions.

The main goal of the Sarbanes-Oxley Act is to protect investors and increase their confidence in public companies. Specific measures of the Act require that a company's CEO and CFO each certify quarterly and annually that:

- He or she reviewed the report being filed.
- To his or her knowledge, the report does not contain any untrue statements or omit any material facts.
- The financial statements and other financial information fairly present, in all material respects, the financial position, results of operations, and cash flows.
- He or she is responsible for and has designed, established, and maintained Disclosure Controls & Procedures (DC&P), as well as evaluated and reported on the effectiveness of those controls and procedures within 90 days of the report filing date.

Effectively, this means that on a daily basis, the certifying officers need to ensure that systems are set up and monitored sufficiently to satisfy themselves that all disclosure procedures and controls are operating effectively. In its comment on the Act the SEC states:

> "We believe that the purpose of internal controls and procedures for financial reporting is to ensure that companies have processes designed to provide reasonable assurance that: The company's transactions are properly authorized; the company's assets are safeguarded against unauthorized or improper use; and the company's transactions are properly recorded and reported to permit the preparation of the registrant's financial statements in conformity with generally accepted accounting principles."

Although the Sarbanes-Oxley Act has not established specific rules and standards for reporting on internal controls and procedures for financial reporting, it is the responsibility of the CEO, CFO, and CIO to establish these guidelines and manage them diligently to remain in compliance with the Act. Ultimately, this Act guarantees that a Corporation's commitment to transparent and ethical reporting methodology is as important as its commitment to its bottom line; and government, investors, and the public are looking to top executives to make this happen.

EVENTS LEADING UP TO THE ACT

History of Accounting and Financial Reporting Standards

The last major crisis that prompted a serious overhaul of the Accounting and Financial Reporting standards for public companies came after the stock market crash of 1929. The crash resulted in vast investor losses and the subsequent financial depression. Washington's response was to establish the Securities and Exchange Commission (SEC) by the Securities Act of 1933 and the Securities Exchange Act of 1934. The SEC was given statutory authority to set accounting standards and oversight over the activities of auditors. The role of establishing auditing standards was left to the accounting profession.

The accounting profession formed a series of committees that between 1938 and 1959 issued fifty-one authoritative pronouncements that formed the basis of what is now known as generally accepted accounting principles, or GAAP. Today, the Financial Accounting Standards Board (FASB) sets the ground rules for measuring, reporting, and disclosing information in financial statements of non-governmental entities. These accounting standards cover a wide range of topics- everything from broad concepts such as revenue and income recognition, to more specific rules such as how to report information about the company's different businesses. The SEC officially recognizes the FASB's accounting standards as authoritative.

Regulation Overhaul

For the past sixty years the US accounting profession's system of self-regulation including Peer review, a Public Oversight Board (POB), Quality Control Inquiry Committee (QCIC), Professional Ethics Division, and Continuing Professional Education (CPE) has helped create the most respected financial markets in the world.

Then the plight of Enron spurned a public debate over the effectiveness and ethics of the financial accounting, reporting, and auditing processes.

On December 2, 2001, less than a month after it admitted accounting errors that inflated earnings by almost $600 million since 1994, Enron Corporation filed for bankruptcy protection. With $62.8 billion in assets, it became the largest bankruptcy case in U.S. history. The day Enron filed for bankruptcy, its stock closed at 72 cents, more than $75 less than a year earlier. Many employees lost their life savings and tens of thousands of investors lost billions. Shortly after this, WorldCom, crippled by $41 billion in debt and a recent disclosure that it hid $3.9 billion in expenses, filed for bankruptcy protection with $107 billion in assets, making it the largest bankruptcy ever filed in the US.

Government Reaction

On July 30, 2002, President George W. Bush signed into law the Sarbanes-Oxley Act of 2002; the most dramatic change to federal securities laws since the 1930s. The Act dramatically redesigns federal regulations regarding corporate governance and reporting obligations of public companies. It also significantly tightens accountability standards for directors, top executives including the CEO, CFO, and CIO, auditors, securities analysts and legal counsel.

The Act is organized into eleven titles dealing with auditor independence, corporate responsibility, enhanced financial disclosures, conflicts of interest and corporate accountability, among other things.

Components of the Sarbanes-Oxley Act

COMPONENTS	SECTIONS
Title I Public Company Accounting Oversight	101 - 109
Title II Auditor Independence	201 – 209

KEY COMPONENTS OF THE ACT

Sections 301-308 dealing with Corporate Responsibility and Sections 401-409 dealing with Enhanced Financial Disclosures are the most compelling sections and the ones that have received the most attention and analysis. Section 302, pertaining to disclosure controls and procedures and Section 404, pertaining to internal controls and procedures for financial reporting are the two sections that are most relevant and have received the most scrutiny.

Section 302 mandates that with each quarterly filing, The CEO and CFO must each certify that they have evaluated the accuracy and effectiveness of the corporation's internal controls. In addition, they must disclose all significant deficiencies, material weaknesses, and acts of fraud. Section 906 also requires certification of the financial reports in a separate document. Section 404 requires an annual evaluation of internal controls and procedures of financial reporting and auditing. Under these provisions, a company must document its internal control mechanisms that have a direct impact on its financial reporting, evaluate them for compliance, and disclose any gaps and deficiencies. To add further controls, an independent auditor must issue a written report that attests to management's certification on the effectiveness of its internal financial and audit controls, its procedures, and financial reporting.

For the first time in history, failure to comply with the certification and disclosure requirements can and will result in personal criminal liability (steep fines and/or imprisonment) for the executives involved. According to the new legislation, "corporate negligence is equally sanctionable as deliberate malfeasance."

Key Specific Regulations

Section 101: Public Company Accounting Oversight Board (PCAOB) Membership

The Board shall consist of five full-time members (two CPAs and three non-CPAs) who are all financially literate. No member of the Board can be receiving payment or share in the profit of any public accounting firm other than retirement benefits or other fixed payments. The Chair may not have practiced as a CPA within the previous five years.

Section 103: PCAOB's Duties

The Board is responsible for:

- Setting the budget and managing its operations
- Establishing "auditing, quality control, ethics, independence, and other standards relating to the preparation of audit reports for issuers"
- Registering and inspecting accounting firms
- Investigating irregularities and imposing appropriate sanctions
- Enforcing compliance with the Act and other laws or standards relating to the preparation and issuance of audit reports
- Performing other duties as required

The Board must adopt an audit standard to implement the internal control review required by section 404.

Section 105: PCAOB Investigations

Information received or prepared by the Board shall be "confidential and privileged as an evidentiary matter (and shall not be subject to civil discovery other legal process) in any proceeding in any Federal or State court or administrative agency, unless and until presented in connection with a public proceeding or [otherwise] released." No sanctions report will be made available to the public unless and until stays pending appeal have been lifted.

Section 107(d): PCAOB Sanctions

The SEC has the right to require the Board to carry out additional responsibilities such as keeping certain records, and it can inspect the Board as necessary.

Section 107(c): Review of Disciplinary Action Taken By the PCAOB

The SEC can change, cancel, reduce, or increase sanctions applied by the Board.

Section 108: Accounting Standards

The SEC recognizes GAAP and all the principles therein, and any new procedures must adhere to the GAAP principles.

Section 201: Prohibited Activities of Professional Service Providers

The firm that supplies auditing services to a client cannot provide (1) bookkeeping or other accounting record service to the audit client; (2) financial information systems design and implementation; (3) appraisal or valuation services; (4) actuarial services; (5) internal audit outsourcing services; (6) management functions or human resources; (7) brokerage, investment adviser, or investment banking services; (8) legal services; (9) any other service that the Board determines, by regulation, is impermissible.

Section 206: Conflict of Interest

The CEO, Controller, CFO, etc. cannot have worked for the audit firm in the year previous to the audit.

Section 301: Public Company Audit Committees

The audit committee is to be made up of Board members who are guaranteed to be independent and free of conflicting interests with the corporation.

Section 302: Certification

CEOs and CFOs must certify in each reporting period that the information presented is accurate and fairly represents the financial position of the company and operational results. Certifying officers will face penalties for false certification of $1,000,000 and/or up to 10 years' imprisonment for "knowing" of a violation and $5,000,000 and/or up to 20 years' imprisonment for "willing" a violation.

Section 304: Forfeiture of Certain Bonuses and Profits

If an issuer is required to prepare an accounting restatement due to the material noncompliance of the issuer, as a result of misconduct, with any financial reporting requirement under the securities laws, the chief executive officer and chief financial officer of the issuer shall reimburse the issuer for any bonus or other incentive-based or equity-based compensation received by that person from the issuer during the 12-month period following the first public issuance or filing with the Commission (whichever first occurs) of the financial document embodying such financial reporting requirement; and any profits realized from the sale of securities of the issuer during that 12-month period.

Section 306: Blackout Periods

Officers and directors and other insiders may not purchase or sell stock during blackout periods.

Section 401(a): Disclosures in Periodic Reports

All financial reports are to be prepared according to GAAP and shall "reflect all material correcting adjustments . . . that have been identified by a registered accounting firm . . . ."

Section 401 (c): Off-Balance Sheet Disclosures
The SEC shall study off-balance sheet disclosures to determine the extent of the transaction and whether GAAP rules were applied such that the transactions are transparent to investors.

Section 402: Prohibition of Personal Loans to Executives
No public company, except consumer credit institutions, may loan or renew a loan of a personal nature to its executive officers or directors. A credit company may issue consumer loans and credit cards to its directors and executive officers if it is done in the ordinary course of business on the same terms and conditions made to the general public.

Section 403: Disclosures of Insider Trades
Directors, officers, and 10% owners must report insider trades within two business days of the transaction.

Section 404: Internal Controls
Management must state their responsibility in establishing, maintaining, and analyzing the internal control structure and make an assessment of the effectiveness of such processes.

Section 406: Codes of Ethics
A corporation is required to have a Code of Ethics that addresses financial data and record integrity. If a corporation does not have a Code of Ethics they must justify their position.

Section 407: Financial Expert
At least one member of the audit committee must be a "financial expert;" a person who has education and

experience as a public accountant, auditor, principal financial officer, controller or principal accounting officer.

Section 409: Real Time Disclosure
Issuers must disclose information on material changes in the financial condition or operations of the issuer on a rapid and current basis.

Title VIII: Corporate and Criminal Fraud
- It is a felony to "knowingly" obstruct a federal investigation by tampering with documents or other such actions.
- Auditors are required to maintain records for five years.
- Section 806 - Employees are given "whistleblower protection" that prohibits the employer from taking retaliatory action against employees who disclose information relevant to a fraud claim.

Title IX: White Collar Crime
- Maximum penalty for mail and wire fraud is increased from 5 to 10 years.
- Tampering with a record or otherwise obstructing a proceeding is a crime.
- A CEO or CFO who knowingly or willfully certifies financial reports that are misleading faces a fine up to $5,000,000 and/or imprisonment of up to 20 years.

Section 1102: Tampering With a Record
It a crime to alter, destroy, or conceal any document with the intent to obstruct an official proceeding with a penalty of up to 20 years in prison and a fine.

Section 1105: Prohibited Board Members
A person who has committed securities fraud may be prohibited by the SEC from serving as a Board member.

IMPACT OF THE ACT

The Sarbanes-Oxley Act of 2002 requires public companies to validate the accuracy and integrity of their financial management. The processes and documentation required for compliance are rigorous and require a commitment from all members of the organization. From the CEO to the accounting clerk to the information specialist, all employees must operate using ethical and accurate standards and those standards must be communicated through, and reinforced by, the corporate culture.

Sarbanes-Oxley and Corporate Culture

It is one thing to create new laws and regulations and expect companies to follow them, but it is an entirely different matter to efficiently implement those changes; that is where corporate culture comes into play. The "tone from the top" is a crucial element in achieving change of this magnitude and importance.

The message prior to Sarbanes-Oxley was primarily profit driven; now corporate communication needs to emphasize setting realistic expectations and goals for the company and staff. That means from setting sales targets to planning budgets, all goals need to be fundamentally achievable without cutting corners or concealing information. Crucial to this process is managers who walk the talk and encourage open lines of communication between management and staff.

To ensure open communication, ethics programs need to be implemented and followed. No longer a gratuitous function of the Human Resource department, ethics programs will serve as the intermediary where employees can report suspected misconduct without fear of penalty or reprisal. Section 301 of the Sarbanes-Oxley Act requires each audit committee of a public company to establish procedures for the receipt of confidential and anonymous submissions by employees regarding questionable accounting or auditing matters. Section 806 requires corporations to set up a formal "whistle blowing" program that protects the anonymity of the informant and protects them from reprisals. Employees must understand corporate rules and regulations and have a clear idea of how their role fits within their department and with the overall mission of the company. It is imperative that all employees feel connected with, and part of, the business.

This connection also means understanding that strict penalties can be imposed on individuals for not properly reporting financial matters throughout the ranks. In order for management to certify the financial information they are presenting to the public is accurate, they will expect their accounting, finance, and information professionals to adhere to the utmost of professional and ethical standards. Managers need to set this example and incorporate a best practices routine for their staff to model. That means taking the time to review documentation, asking questions about the numbers and information sources, and addressing issues as they arise. Rubber stamping is no longer acceptable and due diligence does not indicate distrust in a colleague's work, rather; it reinforces the importance of accurate reporting and attending to issues at the source so that they can be rectified and abated.

Sarbanes-Oxley and the Finance Department

The Finance department will undergo enormous change as Sarbanes-Oxley related reforms roll out. The Act is viewed by many as, primarily, a finance act; while that is not entirely true, finance carries the burden of proving to the rest of the company, the Board, the Auditors, and the Investors that the corporation is in compliance. Regardless of who sits on the committees or who else makes certifications, when it comes to financial reporting the "go-to" person will be the CFO.

The most obvious and potent change for the CFO is the responsibility status placed on the position. The CFO and the CEO have joint responsibility for certifying that all reports of financial information are accurate and truthful, and that the systems that generated the reports are effective and reliable. The CFO no longer has one more chain of command to report to in terms of information integrity; his or her neck is on the line with liability equal to the CEO.

Even if the CFO had always considered himself/herself as second-in-command anyway, now there is no doubt that the stakes of the position have been raised. The added pressure of this level of responsibility and accountability is daunting at best and terrifying at worst. The whole transacting, data recording, data manipulating, report-generating machine is in need of a tune-up or major overhaul and the consequences of failure involve personal, criminal liability. The role of CFO will be integral and highly influential in the change process.

Change management is discussed often enough but the fact is, for many companies, changes to get in line with Sarbanes-Oxley will be the most significant they have ever experienced. Change of this magnitude requires paramount leadership ability and as a leader in this process, the CFO will need a big bag of tricks. The sheer number and diversity of people that must be involved in the process will make for very lively discussion in the conference rooms, halls, offices, and cubicles throughout the corporation. Many executives think of change as an organizational dynamic that the HR department deals with; to keep from being steamrolled in this process, the CFO requires some change management skills of his own.

To mange change, the people in charge have to be leaders in all senses of the word. Visionary, inspiring, motivating, dedicated – all those qualities will be necessary for the CFO and the compliance team to accomplish its task. It will also require a great deal of confidence in fellow team members to carry out their duties and to delegate duties to. Likely, the CFO will be working closely with people they previously had little contact with. The IT department is the most obvious inclusion in this group, but HR, Marketing and Sales, and heads of SBUs may also be unfamiliar teammates. The divergent nature of the cross-functional team will present many challenges and opportunities for all members of the organization to gain an understanding and appreciation of the value each department brings to the table. Because Sarbanes-Oxley reform goes way beyond finance and essentially dictates a new way of doing business, the corporation has a prime opportunity and responsibility to make the most of the changes.

To institute broad-sweeping, corporate-wide reform will take a concerted effort from all departments and the CFO will be thrust into a main leadership role. Aside from personal liability, the CFO will have high visibility in the process and this is the perfect venue to prove (or disprove) his or her leadership ability. The CFO will have to transform the entire finance department into a transparent and team-oriented unit; unfortunately, this will be quite a leap for many. The finance department will be looked at as a model for the new and open atmosphere that is necessary for the data integrity and accuracy demanded by Sarbanes-Oxley.

To ensure dependable data and transparent operations, it will be necessary to shift the focus of Finance from the department that controls the money to the department that ensures forthrightness. Rather than being seen as the gatekeeper of the money and the approver of expenses, the CFO will need to establish an environment that is forgiving of over-budgets and understanding of unforeseen expenses. These are the situations that drive many of the less-than-accurate transactions that are recorded and are what motivate otherwise honest managers to "fudge" the numbers a little. Of additional concern are HR policies that rely on aggressive financial and sales targets for pay incentive programs. All of the executives, the Board, and corporate programs will need to embrace the new idea of operational integrity by supporting the CFO and communicating the message to the employees.

Because all data recording processes eventually entail human intervention, the best way to mitigate dishonesty is to remove the motivators. The CEO and the CFO have added motivation to ensure this occurs because Sarbanes-Oxley sets out very foreboding, personal consequences for them if the system fails. Sarbanes-Oxley sections that impact the CFO directly include:

- CEOs and CFOs are required to certify all reports that contain financial statements.
- CEOs and CFOs are required to certify both annual and quarterly reports. Furthermore, they must

certify that all facts in the annual report are true and no information or facts have been left out.

- Those CEOs or CFOs found to violate the rule, who must restate its financial information, will lose any bonuses and all other incentives for the one-year period prior to the first filing of the misleading financial information.
- It is the responsibility of CEOs and CFOs to identify, establish, and maintain internal controls, making sure they are apprised of all material information.
- Any CEO, CFO or other individual found to have destroyed, falsified or changed records after a company declares bankruptcy or during a federal investigation may be fined, imprisoned for up to 20 years, or both.

These responsibilities and sanctions directly discourage the top two sources of fraudulent human intervention and it is their responsibility to drive down the tenets of honestly, integrity and ethics to the rest of the company.

The CFO can approach Sarbanes-Oxley with negativity, viewing it as a migraine headache on steroids; or, he or she can embrace the revolutionary reforms as a perfect opportunity to grow the profession and improve American corporations. The fall-out bonuses include a richer understanding of the corporation and all its departments, an opportunity to drive up the value of finance, and reap the many benefits that come with increased responsibility and respect.

Sarbanes-Oxley and the IT Department

Sarbanes-Oxley, the new financial reporting law, likely means huge changes to information systems technology. One of the principal ways that corporations and corporate executives can reduce their corporate, and now personal, liabilities is to implement changes to the IT infrastructures that support the compliance and disclosure demands of Sarbanes-Oxley. Some industry analysts are saying that bringing systems into compliance with the Act may overshadow the time and expense invested in the Y2K fixes. Addressing Y2K was a single task but the changes necessary to achieve Sarbanes-Oxley compliance are expected to take place on an evolutionary basis as the systems are updated and integrated. Even companies whose systems appear to comply with the Act are uncertain as to exactly what some provisions mean; ultimately, it may mean costly overhauls to budgeting, reporting, and decision-support systems across the board. The result is that many companies are expecting to implement major systems changes related to governance and compliance issues.

Corporate responsibility is forefront in the changes mandated by Sarbanes-Oxley. Section 302 requires the CEO and CFO to sign statements verifying the completeness and accuracy of financial reports. This means that executives who are liable at report-signing time will demand systems that are accurate, timely, and tamper-proof. The accuracy demanded will place enormous pressure on the multitude of information systems running in a company. Because this section requires executives to sign off not only on their companies' financial statements, but also on the control processes that surround the collection of the data behind them—down to the transaction level, the IT department will be charged with auditing and verifying each step in a transaction, from order, to payment, to storage of data, to aggregation into financial reports. This will also require a process of monitoring each step and include a procedure to alert key people to breaches in the system. This may mean enhancing current systems or incorporating systems that can enforce business rules and transform data without human intervention or software that can report exceptions and alert internal or external auditors when something goes awry.

While complete tamper proofing is probably impossible, given the fact that a minor error in any of the thousands of processes involved in the system will need to be fixed to ensure accuracy; financial data will need to be made as secure as humanly possible. This will require absolute diligence in creating systems that are secure and manage financial information separate from access to the places where data is stored. Because systems are only as secure as the people who have access to them, users should be limited to those systems that are essential to their job function and only system administrators should maintain the underlying database of information.

Accuracy is one element of the changes required and speed is the other. Section 409 requires that companies report changes in financial condition "on a rapid and current basis" and that they have systems for "real-time disclosure." Sarbanes-Oxley significantly reduces the time allowed to file reports:

- Quarterly reports must be filed within 35 days of quarter-end (down from 45 days) by 2005.
- Annual reports must be filed within 60 days of year-end (down from 75 days) by 2005.
- Disclosure of "material events" and insider trades must be filed within two days.

The speed of a system and its integration processes must be able to keep up with these rigorous information demands. Older systems such as legacy Cobol-based transaction processing systems or terminal-based order entry systems will not allow for such fast processing and "flat-file" batches or other periodic data transfer methods may hamper efficient integration.

Those companies that have been proactive with financial–consolidation software systems have likely focused on integrating budget, reports, planning and analysis tools. The means that many of the systems needed to provide a complete view of the operation's functions will have been left out. Financial data and non-financial indicators will need to be interfaced in order to provide the detail that the SEC requires under Sarbanes-Oxley. In order to accomplish this task, many internal processes will have to be put in place to facilitate it. Essentially, an entire organization will require change and the organization will expect IT to lead, not hinder, the way.

This is a huge undertaking and one that will involve many man hours and sometimes, prohibitive budgets. The accuracy of the reports coming out is an absolute requirement and a great deal of money will be spent accomplishing that objective; the issue of tightening the timeframe for reporting will put an even greater pressure on IT resources stretched thin by these other commitments. While large companies will just have to find the money and other resources somewhere; smaller companies that are still relying on spreadsheet-based solutions face huge obstacles and costs that have the potential to effect business operations and efficiencies.

Sarbanes-Oxley will require radical changes to the manner and speed of information flow within the corporation: IT and its value position will change forever.

Financial system overhauls will need to address all the control, monitoring, and reporting processes of a company, meaning that a top-to-bottom examination of any and all systems from inventory control to payroll will be required. IT departments and the company will likely face higher labor costs as they prepare to meet the compliance regulations and then maintain the systems afterward. Requests for system changes will likely come fast and often and projects that may have seemed unjustifiable from a cost benefit standpoint in the past will likely take on a new significance under Sarbanes-Oxley rules.

As daunting as the task of overhauling a company's IT system is, the CIO faces an even stronger legal hazard from the rollout of the Sarbanes-Oxley Act. As it becomes more and more apparent that IT is an integral link in the financial reporting system, CIOs will likely be held to the same liability standards as CEOs and CFOs when it comes to assuring the accuracy of reports. HealthSouth's CIO Kenneth Livesay was fired and pleaded guilty in April 2003 to federal charges of falsifying financial information and conspiracy to commit wire and securities fraud. He and seven other financial employees including the CFO and Chief Controller have admitted their guilt in the scheme to artificially inflate HealthSouth earnings and assets during the past several years. The information coming out is only as good as the information going in, and the onus will be on the IT department to ensure data integrity, reliability, and accuracy.

Sarbanes-Oxley and Corporate Management

Despite the grumbling about the cost to deploy systems that will enable corporations to comply with Sarbanes-Oxley initiated reforms, the consensus among senior executives it that the outcome will benefit the company as much as the investors. By leveraging the controls put in place under Sarbanes-Oxley, corporations will have much more accurate and timely data with which to make all business decisions. Benefits of this process include:

- Improved flow of information allowing better business decisions
- Better management of resources
- Streamlined operations
- Improved investor relations
- Enhanced reputation for integrity and reliable financial reporting

The notion that accurate and timely data will improve operating efficiency is certainly not new, and the issue of transparent and ethical treatment of business data has always been lauded. Sarbanes-Oxley is the catalyst that has brought all these elements to the forefront; out from theoretical posturing and into actual solutions. All three factors will work together to ultimately create stronger corporations that have greater sustainability in economic downturns.

Accurate data is an obvious necessity when making any business decision, from the mundane to the momentous. Senior management will need to instill this into every employee and every process so that accuracy is paramount to on-budget. This certainly does not mean a reckless use of assets is required to maintain accurate records, it simply means that the generally accepted business practice (GABP) is to choose the most accurate method rather than the cheapest method. This will mean a shift in focus for many corporations across all industries and of all sizes; however, the long-term benefits will outweigh the initial costs.

Second to accurate information is the need for timely information. Accurate figures are most useful when they can be used to determine future practices rather than analyze historic events. With periodic reports coming out weeks and months after the closing date, many business decisions are made using insufficient forecasts and outdated information. Linking day-to-day operations with anticipated results will enable the management team to identify and react to divergences much quicker and much more effectively. Many hours are put into strategic planning and timely information is key to keeping the corporation on course.

There will be little argument that timely and accurate data improves business efficiency and transparency is the third factor that will ensure operational sustenance. Transparent accounting and reporting is the key to investor satisfaction and investors will ultimately keep the corporation healthy and prosperous. Investors want to have confidence that the information presented to them is historically correct, currently relevant, and future oriented. The difficulty will be in aligning these factors and bringing them together at the same time – to meet Sarbanes-Oxley requirements and to meet future regulatory and economic challenges.

Compliance Committee

Integral to bringing this compliance effort to fruition will be an empowered, capable and diverse compliance committee. The CEO in small to mid-size organizations and the CFO or other designate in larger corporations will likely chair this committee. It will be extremely important to include the CIO and other key information and technology staff because IT solutions will drive most of the changes required to achieve compliance reporting. This committee will identify and spearhead the reform movement and it will be extremely important that the whole organization know and understand the purpose and function of the committee and its authority to lead change.

In order to be effective, this compliance committee should team with other risk management functions in the organization. This will broaden the perspective and give the various departments or business units the opportunity to contribute their expertise. The internal auditors will certainly be able to suggest many effective ways to identify and monitor areas that require attention. Manufacturing and Sales will be able to alert the committee to potential sources of error that emanate from their departments. Human Resources will be invaluable in the communication and rollout phase and will provide necessary resource support when it comes to actual implementation of the plan. This is a corporate-wide issue and it will require corporate-wide involvement in order to develop new and improved systems for integrating and controlling the flow of information within and outside the company.

Centralized vs. Decentralized Strategy

When attempting change that involves corporate-wide involvement, it will be necessary to employ a more centralized approach to the management of the process. This isn't to imply that Sarbanes-Oxley requires a centralized structure; it does mean that the tenets of centralization, like uniform policies and procedures and hierarchical access controls, will be necessary to assure the CEO and CFO that the reports they are certifying are correct. Improved controls usually mean more or tighter controls and this will be necessary in the new reporting environment. It will be a fine line between control and autonomy.

While the pendulum keeps swinging on the centralized vs. decentralized debate, the key factor in successful implementation of these new corporate governance standards will be the acceptance by line and staff employees. The control systems put in place are only as trustworthy as the people who operate within them. Taking away too much autonomy alienates staff and giving them too much discretion and access creates too many risks. This is again where the "tone from the top" figures in; the Board, the Executives and the Compliance Committee will need to communicate changes effectively and openly and create systems that employees will embrace and that will not create operational inefficiency or unnecessary burdens.

PROCESSES OR SYSTEMS?

The short answer: Both. To further convolute the situation, the question of which will drive the other is analogous to the chicken and the egg argument. Sarbanes-Oxley requires a shift in governance focus. Bottom-line is second to honesty. Stakeholders will no longer tolerate incorrect, misleading, or fraudulent information or activity and this requires reform that will cover business processes and control systems. As the two areas that drive how corporations operate and how employees make decisions, they are inextricably intertwined and changes in one will spur changes in the other and vice versa. The important thing to keep in mind throughout the reform is that the intention of Sarbanes-Oxley is to improve.

Analyzing business processes at the micro-level was not seen as a cost-effective activity prior to this legislation. As a result, there are likely a plethora of inefficiencies and unnecessary activities that go on daily because "that is just how it has always been." The processes and procedures can now be looked at from an effectiveness standpoint and the systems can be analyzed for integrity; the opportunity to gain operational efficiency is enormous. Process deficiencies will lead to system failures and system failures will require unnecessary or redundant processes. Sarbanes-Oxley unwittingly (or perhaps purposefully?) gives corporations "permission" to examine their operations and forgives the potential income losses related to the initial expenses of compliance.

For Sarbanes-Oxley to achieve the largest impact, the smallest components of the organization require attention. While much of the Act focuses on and discusses control systems, it is important to remember that systems and processes function together. The best controls can be put in place, but if operational processes do not support the new system, employees will act based on method not control. In the medium to long term, improved processes and systems will lead to improved corporate function and ultimately lead to more satisfied investors; a large feat based on the compound effect of many small process and system changes.

CONSEQUENCES OF NONCOMPLIANCE

Human nature being what it is, the Act seeks to ensure compliance through harsh sanctions. Sarbanes-Oxley creates new or broader federal crimes for obstruction of justice and securities fraud, with maximum prison time of 20 or 25 years, respectively. Sentences for many existing federal crimes were enhanced. Mail and wire fraud maximum penalties were quadrupled, from 5 to 20 years. The maximum sentence for some securities law violations was doubled from 10 to 20 years, and the maximum fine against a company for the same offense was increased from $2.5 million to $25 million.

The strength of the criminal penalties portion of Sarbanes-Oxley will depend on the government's success in prosecuting specific individuals. The statute's harsher penalties cannot be applied to crimes committed prior to the laws' passing, so only time will tell their true effectiveness. For Sarbanes-Oxley to have the bite intended, corporate officers (considered the prime perpetrators of corporate scandal) are expected to have to serve prison time in addition to the hefty fines imposed.

Civil and Criminal Penalties

According to the Sarbanes-Oxley Act of 2002 and New York City Office of the Comptroller:

Action	Penalty
Altering, destroying, or concealing any records with the intent of obstructing a federal investigation.	Fine and/or up to 10 years imprisonment.
Failure to maintain audit or review "workpapers" for at least five years.	Fine and/or up to 5 years imprisonment.
Anyone who "knowingly executes, or attempts to execute, a scheme" to defraud a purchaser of securities.	Fine and/or up to 10 years imprisonment.

CEO or CFO who "recklessly" violates his or her certification of the company's financial statements.	Fine of up to $1mm and/or up to 10 years imprisonment.
If the violation is "willful", then the penalty increases.	Fine of up to $5 mm and/or up to 20 years.
Conspiracy by two or more persons to commit any offense against, or to defraud the U.S. or its agencies.	Fine and/or up to 10 years imprisonment.
Any person who "corruptly" alters, destroys, conceals, etc., any records or documents with the intent of impairing the integrity of the record or document for use in an official proceeding.	Fine and/or up to 20 years imprisonment.
Mail and wire fraud.	Penalty increase from 5 to 20 years imprisonment.
Violating applicable Employee Retirement Income Security Act (ERISA) provisions.	Various lengths depending on violation.

CHAPTER 1
SCOPE AND ASSESSMENT OF THE ACT

There are some pervasive themes that emerge from the Sarbanes-Oxley Act. The Act is built on the following basic and key principles:

Integrity
The process of reporting and disclosing material information to stakeholders must be honest and truthful. The stability of the US market depends on investor trust in the corporations and the systems in which they operate; Sarbanes-Oxley is the means to guarantee trust and integrity.

Independence
For a system to function reliably it must have a certain degree of autonomy. For corporations, this means that the people entrusted to ensure fair and accurate representation must be impartial and independent. The auditors and board members must be free to operate objectively and in the best interests of investors to maintain stability in, and accuracy of, corporate reporting.

Proper Oversight
Guidance and supervision are key elements at any level of management and that means that the Executives (CEO, CFO, CIO, COO), the Board and the Auditors need to have explicit means to evaluate the effectiveness of their governance and compliance systems. This means ensuring that all systems are linked and that all departments and functions have effective methods of sharing compliance information.

Accountability
All stakeholders, from investors to employees to customers, deserve accountability from the executives who manage the corporation they have a vested interest in.

Accountability breeds responsibility and the tough, new standards of the Sarbanes-Oxley Act ensure someone is held accountable for the daily operations of the company and disclosure of the company's performance.

Strong Internal Controls

For any system to be effective it requires assiduous control systems. Internal controls are the measures against which corporate effectiveness is judged. Essentially, controls are the framework that an auditor will use to determine your compliance, and Sarbanes-Oxley makes it absolutely necessary for corporations to design and implement explicit, effective internal controls that will guarantee that compliance.

Transparency

The corporation's movements must be open to scrutiny from all angles. When all transactions are subject to public disclosure, transparency of the system acts as its own control system. Sarbanes-Oxley mandates transparent operations, which enhance corporate responsibility and governance.

Deterrence

Unfortunately, corporate executives, officials, and employees are human and that means suitable and significant deterrents are required in order to discourage behavior that is unacceptable. Sarbanes-Oxley has introduced strong, new measures that introduce harsher penalties for white-collar crime and criminalize activity intended to obstruct justice or commit securities fraud.

CORPORATE PROCESS MANAGEMENT

Who is best suited to ramp-up for Sarbanes-Oxley compliance? Is it the CFO, the CIO, both or neither?

Who Leads?
Joe, the CFO at BOLO Corporation has been charged with implementing the changes necessary to

comply with Sarbanes-Oxley and the new regulations imposed by the SEC. The current financial systems rely on spreadsheet solutions and after much research, Joe has decided that the financial information must be consolidated and the whole process sped up. He knows he will need IT support to create the changes necessary and provide the software and hardware, but he is confident he can design a control system framework that IT can work with. He doesn't want to bother the CIO with his finance problems related to Sarbanes-Oxley, so he goes about the process of creating a wonderful, theoretical system that will allow information to flow through the company accurately and quickly. He presents his findings to the CEO, who is delighted, but when it comes times for application, the CIO comes up with many "excuses" for why the plan is not practical or doable. "Trust IT to always be the cog in the wheel" he says.

This notion of IT's "irrelevance" is at the core of who is best suited to lead the Sarbanes-Oxley challenge. The CIO is the keeper of the corporate data and it is the IT systems that will determine how financial information is recorded, tracked and disclosed yet many executives (CIOs included) view compliance with Sarbanes-Oxley as a finance issue, not a systems issue. Some recognize that IT has a role to play, but the focus is still on the finance department to lead the way.

These executives are gravely mistaken. Sarbanes-Oxley is financial legislation, but its implementation and compliance issues rest with the IT department. Sarbanes-Oxley requires a sophisticated set of internal controls that guide the creation of financial documents and disclosure of financial information in a timely and accurate manner. Since IT systems are used to generate, change, house and transport that data, CIOs have to build the controls that ensure the information stands up to audit scrutiny.

If CIOs are considered ancillary to the process, how will the necessary systems be developed and controls put in place? It is imperative that IT is an integral component of Sarbanes-Oxley compliance and as such, the

CIO will need to demonstrate a thorough understanding of the issues related to Sarbanes-Oxley. CFOs may resist letting the technology department play a central role in implementing the necessary changes to ensure data integrity. From finance's perspective, IT is a cost center and therefore the CFO needs to manage this process in terms of value to the corporation and not simply spending money on some requisite system upgrades. The CIO is in the unique position of understanding the importance of stringent controls and the functional difficulties of attaining them. Finance and IT are bound in this process and it is important that the corporation enables the two departments to work together to address the challenges of Sarbanes-Oxley.

Aside: The idea that a 404 is a clueless person (as in a 404 message meaning "file not found") is rapidly being replaced by the notion that a 404 means you need to find the information fast to comply with section 404 of Sarbanes-Oxley.

Companies spend an enormous amount of time developing business plans and forecasts on which to base important decisions. It is critical that the information that drives their strategic decision-making is accurate and timely. A 2003 survey by the Hackett Group concluded that 47 percent of companies used standalone spreadsheets for planning and budgeting. Considering the importance that is placed on the information that comes out of these spreadsheets, it is alarming that a study by Rajalingham, Chadwick and Knight (2000) found that 90% of the spreadsheets analyzed had significant errors. Actual or potential spreadsheet error will be unacceptable to CEOs and CFOs who must personally certify the information in financial reports to be true.

A critical challenge for Sarbanes-Oxley compliance will be to reduce the reliance on human processes in the flow of information and record management. This responsibility falls firmly on IT's shoulders and the CIO will have to document usage rules and an audit trail for each system that contributes financial information. CIOs need to work closely with the Sarbanes-Oxley auditors to make sure that they know what their

30

companies' weaknesses are and then take immediate action to remedy the situation.

ANALYST'S OPINIONS AND RECOMMENDATIONS

According to analysts, to meet compliance, companies will want to:

- Determine whether the members of the audit committee and the majority of the board of directors meet the definition of "independent."
- Review the existing code of ethics, making changes to meet act standards, if necessary.
- Put a code of ethics in place if one does not already exist.
- Determine the financial expertise of the members of the audit committee.
- Ensure that the company's benefit plans comply with restrictions during blackout periods.
- Ensure the non-audit services being performed do not violate Sarbanes-Oxley.
- Ensure that the CFO outlines what information needs to be reported and how quickly it must be reported.
- Ensure that computer technology has the ability to get information to CFOs in a timely fashion.
- Enact a process in which the CFO will be able to inform the IT department of compliance issues in a timely manner.
- Identify internal processes that could possibly pose risks for the company.
- Consider having all directors, officers and their families first go through pre-clearance procedures before conducting transactions.
- Appoint an executive(s) to sign a power of attorney, which will allow him to sign off on reports (Section 16.).
- Appoint disclosure committee, if one isn't already in place, which will help ensure disclosures are

accurate and complete. Appoint an individual from each part of the company, so all departments are covered. Then ensure:

- Everyone understands for what the committee is accountable.
- A committee charter has been written and communicated to appropriate personnel.
- The committee has an agenda.
- All committee members know their specific responsibilities.
- The company is aware of the specific roles of members of the committee.
- Institute a process for resolving disputes between the Disclosure Committee and the CEO and CFO.

- Create a disclosure policy that is tailored specifically to meet the needs of the company.
- Ensure that, if a policy is adopted, it will be adhered to.
- Ensure the company practices and written policies are compatible. If you are doing something in a company practice that is not in the written form, change the written form so that you are in compliance.
- Test the effectiveness of controls and assess how they are doing overall.
- Have an internal audit function in place.
- Create and put into place a process, in compliance with the Whistleblower's mandate, that will allow employees to voice their concerns about possible company violations; this process should also allow them to express their concerns on financial or business practices.
- The executive officers and audit committee should ensure that the internal controls are effective and make efforts to correct any weaknesses.
- Implement dates when completion of strengthening of weaknesses should be completed; also identify the plan of action that will lead to completion.

- Liability insurance and coverage should be inspected to ensure proper coverage and protection.
- CFOs will want to outline, as clearly as possible, the internal processes of financial reports. This will allow the CFO to make determinations on where the company needs to improve its performance to comply with Sarbanes-Oxley.
- According to one analyst, "The level of detail you have to get down to is pretty significant. You have to get down to the level of Excel spreadsheets and determine whether the people using them know what they're doing and whether or not they're being appropriately monitored and reviewed."
- Create a protected hotline that will allow whistleblowers to call in with information.

CHAPTER 2
INTERNAL CONTROLS

Good internal controls are no longer just best practice ...

Internal control means different things to different people. Fortunately, the proposed SEC rule on Section 404 specifically discusses the definition of internal controls offered by COSO, an independent group sponsored by five major accounting organizations, including the American Institute of Certified Public Accountants and the Institute of Internal Auditors.

COSO's definition of **internal control** is:
"a process, effected by an entity's board of directors, management, and other personnel, designed to provide reasonable assurance regarding the achievement of objectives in the following categories:

- effectiveness and efficiency of operations;
- reliability of financial reporting;
- compliance with applicable laws and regulations."

COSO issued a report in 1992 examining corporate fraud and what procedures could be put together to combat it. It recommended that companies adopt a framework whereby all transactions are properly authorized, there are safeguards against improper use, and all transactions are recorded and reported. What that means is that every division in a company needs to have a documented set of internal rules that controls how data is generated, manipulated, recorded, and reported.

In August 2003, the SEC introduced the term **"internal control over financial reporting,"** which is an evolution of the COSO definition specific to Sarbanes-Oxley requirements. Internal control over financial reporting is:

"A process designed by, or under the supervision of, the issuer's principal executive and principal financial officers, or persons performing similar functions, and effected by the issuer's board of directors, management and other personnel, to provide reasonable assurance regarding the reliability of financial reporting and the preparation of financial statements for external purposes in accordance with generally accepted accounting principles and includes those policies and procedures that:

- Pertain to the maintenance of records that in reasonable detail accurately and fairly reflect the transactions and dispositions of the assets of the issuer;
- Provide reasonable assurance that transactions are recorded as necessary to permit preparation of financial statements in accordance with generally accepted accounting principles, and that receipts and expenditures of the issuer are being made only in accordance with authorizations of management and directors of the issuer; and
- Provide reasonable assurance regarding prevention or timely detection of unauthorized acquisition, use or disposition of the issuer's assets that could have a material effect on the financial statements."

The last definition of relevance is the SEC's **Disclosure Controls and Procedures**, which are "designed to ensure that information required to be disclosed by a company in the reports filed by it under the Exchange Act is recorded, processed, summarized, and reported within the time periods specified by the SEC." The disclosures that must be made in order to stay in compliance with Sarbanes-Oxley must be certified just as the internal control systems.

It is apparent that much of the success of compliance with Sarbanes-Oxley hinges on the establishment and management of effective and efficient internal controls and controls that regulate how information is disclosed. Although there is overlap, they are each distinct. Internal control includes such things as signature requirements or periodic data checks whereas a disclosure control relates to ensuring that information required is tracked, recorded, summarized, and reported as required by the SEC.

COMPONENTS OF INTERNAL CONTROL

Internal control consists of five interrelated components that are derived from the way management runs a business, and are integrated with the management process. The components are:

Control Environment

The control environment is the foundation for all other components of internal control. It emanates from the corporate culture and it sets the tone for how employees view control and the way an organization deals with discipline and structure. Control environment factors include:

- Integrity, ethical values, and competence of the employees
- Management philosophy and operating style
- Assignment of authority and responsibility within the organization
- Organizational structure
- Training and development opportunities
- Degree of Board involvement

Because the control environment sets the stage for all other elements of control within an organization, it is the crucial element in determining how effective the internal controls are. The best laid-out system will not survive if the environment it operates in does not support and encourage the various processes and rules.

Risk Assessment

Risk assessment is the identification and analysis of relevant risks to achievement of the objectives and it forms the basis for determining how the risks should be managed. All organizations are subject to internal and external risks that must be continuously assessed. Risk assessment involves identifying and analyzing risks that are relevant to the objectives of the firm and it forms a basis for determining how the identified risks should be managed. Because risks will change with the economic, industrial, regulatory, and operating environments, it is necessary to put mechanisms in place that will identify and deal with the risk of change.

Control Activities

Control activities are the policies and procedures that management develops to ensure its objectives are met and its directives are carried out. They are the rules and regulations that guide employees to complete their tasks and are put in place to maintain consistency and reliability within the organization. Control activities occur throughout the organization and include such things as, approvals, authorizations, verifications, reconciliations, reviews of operating performance, security of assets and segregation of duties.

Information and Communication

Relevant information needs to be gathered and communicated to employees in a timely nature to enable them to perform their duties. Information systems are charged with producing reports for operational, financial, and compliance-related programs and make it possible to run and control the business. Information systems gather internal and external data and assimilate that information into useable reports that are used to determine an appropriate course of action.

All communications must flow freely through the organization so that all employees have a clear understanding of what management expects from the control system and the type of control environment they want to foster. Bottom-up flow is as just as crucial to prevent blockages at certain levels, which has the potential to shut executives out of significant loops. Communication with external suppliers, customers, shareholders, and regulators is also an area that needs regulation and control.

Monitoring

Internal control systems need to be monitored diligently. Ongoing monitoring occurs in the course of operations and includes regular management and supervisory activities, and other actions personnel take in performing their duties. The scope and frequency of evaluations will depend primarily on an assessment of risks and the effectiveness of ongoing monitoring procedures. Internal control deficiencies should be reported upstream, with serious matters reported to top management and the board. Control system development is not a static process and the effectiveness needs to be evaluated over time and adjusted as necessary.

A continuous process of risk assessment, communication, risk management, and evaluation forms an effective Internal Control system. This continuous process ensures that the five components of an internal control system are satisfied and it reinforces the importance of controls to the corporation's infrastructure. "Built in" controls support quality and empowerment initiatives, avoid unnecessary costs, and enable a quick response to changing conditions. All components of internal control are relevant to each other and they must all be present and functioning effectively to conclude that internal control over operations is effective.

THE PURPOSE OF INTERNAL CONTROL

The purpose of internal control is to aid the organization's efforts to achieve its operating goals and objectives and to assist in reliable financial reporting and compliance with regulations set out by law or other external sources. Essentially, a good control system is what leads the organization through its day-to-day operations providing rules or guidelines for activities and identifying risks. Internal control is there for guidance, but it will not ensure absolute success or definite achievement of business goals. The most effective systems are subject to human management and the changing regulatory, economic, and competitive environments.

It is also unfortunate that internal control systems cannot guarantee that financial reports are accurate or that they comply with all regulations. Achievement of these objectives is dependent on things outside the sphere of internal control including judgment errors, simple miscalculations, or plain old human mistakes. The need for an ability to override the system in case of such a mistake also opens the system up to error and corruption.

Roles and Responsibilities

Everyone in an organization has responsibility for internal control:

Management

The CEO is ultimately responsible for the internal control system and he or she must provide leadership and direction to senior managers and review the way they're controlling the business. Senior managers then assign responsibility for establishment of more specific internal control policies and procedures to their employees and the process repeats itself down to the control activities of the line and staff workers.

Board of Directors

Management is accountable to the Board, whose members are objective and know about the organization's activities. A strong and effective Board needs to ensure that management cannot override controls that have been put in place or suppress information that is significant to operations in an attempt to "cover its tracks" or claim ignorance later. This type of diligence requires good communication throughout the corporation, especially upward lines.

Internal Auditors

Internal auditors, by their job description and expertise, play a crucial role in monitoring and evaluating the effectiveness of control systems. It is critical that they have enough autonomy and objectivity to report honestly, meaning they should not be under any undue influence from the executive.

Other Employees

For internal control to be effective, everyone in the organization must take some responsibility for it. Almost every employee will create or manipulate information that is input into a control system and they must be aware and understand the ramifications of making mistakes or poor judgments. It is important that all employees have an avenue of communication to report problems or noncompliance and Sarbanes-Oxley's protection for whistleblowers is an explicit recognition of the importance of this.

DEVELOPING AN INTERNAL CONTROL SYSTEM

Fundamental steps in developing an Internal Control system that addresses the needs of Sarbanes-Oxley are:

1. Establish a Compliance Committee

In order to manage the process of compliance with Sarbanes-Oxley, the corporation will need to develop collaborative committees that involve at a minimum the CEO the CFO and the heads of any distinct Business Units. This Compliance Committee should also consist of executives and/or key staff in Finance, IT, legal, and Internal Audit departments. Depending on the size of the organization, this may not be feasible; the bottom line is to have personnel on the committee who are committed to Sarbanes-Oxley compliance and can take a company-wide perspective when identifying risks and coming up with solutions. The corporation itself should commit to providing a workplace forum that is conducive to a coordinated effort. Relying on email communication will not be sufficient and effective communication and resource deployment will be critical. The Compliance Committee will need to focus on:

- Communicating program objectives and initiatives
- Managing the overall process and activities
- Providing training, assessment resources, and tools as necessary

- Engaging the various departments or business units to identify risks and solutions
- Keeping the goals of the Committee visible and compelling

2. **Assess Risk**

Risk assessment is the process of identifying and analyzing both internal and external risks and threats to achieving identified goals and objectives. It can be performed on any specific process within the organization, at all levels of the organization, and for the organization as a whole. Common sources of risk include the following:

- Changes in operating environment
- New technology
- New or changed information systems
- New employees (executives)
- Rapid growth
- New lines, products, or services
- Corporate Restructuring, Mergers/Acquisitions
- Foreign operations
- Regulatory changes

The process of risk assessment involves the following five key components, which are all inter-related and work together to form a continuous evaluation cycle:

1. Determine control objectives
2. Prioritize requirements
3. Identify risks
4. Determine likelihood of the risk
5. Manage risk

To meet the standards of Sarbanes-Oxley, risk will need to be assessed at the corporate-wide level, as well at the individual application level. The SEC has stated that financial report certification will involve more than just financial data and includes documentation and assessment of the internal control systems. Corporate wide risk assessment will address strategic risks and application-level

42

risk assessment focuses more on the transaction and business process services. These risk assessment levels need to be linked so that a systematic and complete measurement tool can be developed that addresses all of the control points and objectives

Control objectives are the specific goals that the corporation wants to achieve at all levels; from the organization as a whole to the specific applications. Examples of control objectives that will meet Sarbanes-Oxley compliance include:

- Satisfactory business planning and needs analysis
- Confidentiality and integrity of transaction systems
- Satisfactory information accuracy and speed of access
- Reliable, valid, authorized, and timely transaction processing
- Proper system implementation and integration
- Satisfactory end-user support and training
- Satisfactory systems and data protection

3.   **Set Reporting Objectives**

After thoroughly analyzing the risks and developing control objectives, it is necessary to determine the likelihood of error and then set decision rules and reporting objectives to address the potential risk. If a control activity is deemed necessary, then it should be the most cost effective and least likely to disrupt operational efficiency. The specific elements of internal control need to be recorded in an official policies and procedures manual and should not only articulate the specific practices the entity employs to achieve its control objectives, but the enforcement policies as well. The following types of controls are the most common and most effective:

- Preventative (stop), detective (catch), and corrective (fix) controls
- Personnel Controls:
  - Separation of duties
  - Careful hiring, assignment of duties, training, and supervision

- o   Performance reviews
- System and Resource Controls:
  - o   Physical controls - access to hardware components of system
  - o   Logistic controls - access and authorization to system
  - o   System controls - document order, internal validity, checks and balances

Corporate wide control focuses on the directives and support that upper management provides to achieve established goals. These controls make it possible for the corporation to be successful and its employees to be productive. The following strategic planning controls are examples for Sarbanes-Oxley compliance:

- Establishing steering committees
- Identifying opportunities provided by enterprise ERP systems
- Evaluating and balancing the level of skills and outside resources required to complete IT projects satisfactorily
- Evaluating automated systems for internal control

Specific Business/Transactions Services Controls include:

- Policies and procedures
- Document validation and matching
- Transaction detail calculation
- Account summary comparison
- Periodic ledger reconciliations
- Help and incident reporting and support
- Management reports

4.   **Prepare a Formal Implementation Plan**
This component includes the identification, capture, and exchange of information in a form and time frame that enables personnel to carry out their responsibilities. It can incorporate methods to record,

process, summarize, and report the entity's transactions, events, and conditions in order to maintain accountability for each respective control activity. A direct and systematic reporting process through the various chains and lines of command must be established, as well as a means of providing an understanding of individual roles and responsibilities in the organization.

5.   **Communicate the Procedures**
Communication is the key to any successful change or management endeavor and compliance with Sarbanes-Oxley may be one of the biggest changes a corporation has faced. The Compliance Committee is responsible for managing the communication process and, since Sarbanes-Oxley will likely require increased control measures, it will be important to emphasize the "why" associated with the changes. Because the success of internal control ultimately relies on each and every employee's performance, the new procedures must be presented clearly and effectively with as much input into the process at lower levels as possible. If only one corporate communiqué gets "buy-in" from the masses, Sarbanes-Oxley is it. All the more reason to focus on collaboration and setting a cultural "tone" that will facilitate employee understanding, acceptance, and observance.

6.   **Provide Training**
Once a system is developed and tested, it will require varying degrees of training to be implemented. Again, the Compliance Committee will lead this process and provide the resources that all employees will need to function successfully in the new environment. The training efforts will consist of internal and external components depending on what type of system is put in place. Sophisticated, pre-packaged IT solutions may require intensive training at various levels and it will be the committee's responsibility to secure the training necessary. The training program created should address internal policies, procedures and practices to ensure each is being performed correctly including:

- Classifying and recording authorized transactions in the proper period
- Operational and financial disclosures
- Protecting company assets from improper, unauthorized use

Through this process, some employee's jobs will change very little and others will require whole new job descriptions. The committee will need to apprise management to be aware of these changes and make personnel decisions accordingly; increased responsibility may lead to promotions, pay increases, and the like and the HR function will need to be managed effectively to eliminate any staff dissatisfaction or inequity; prime sources of risk.

7. **Document Processes and Risk Management**

To comply with section 404, the CEO and CFO will need to certify that the internal controls systems of the corporation are sufficient and that they have been monitored within 90 days of the report being filed. To do this with any degree of confidence, the controls need to be documented diligently. All systems will require detailed descriptions and analysis; clear enough that any audit of the system can be conducted easily and efficiently. Additionally, risks will need to be documented both as a resource for why the controls were put in place and to assist in identification of new or changing sources of risk.

As part of the reporting process, the SEC mandates that a company must maintain "evidential matter" including documentation, to provide reasonable support for management's claim that the internal control system is effective. It is important to remember that that the CEO and CFO are responsible for, or directly supervising, the design of the internal control system relating to financial reporting. Tracking, documenting and analyzing every stage of the process will make the internal control report easier to process and easier for top executives to sign.

8. **Perform Continuous Evaluation**

The quality of the internal control process needs to be continuously evaluated and modified to fit the corporation's changing environment and needs. Detection and timeliness of response are two key factors in maintaining and monitoring a system of internal controls. It is management's responsibility to establish and maintain controls to ensure that they operate as intended or are modified as appropriate.

Early analysis, including detection and resolution of problems, can develop as a reactive process and ultimately develop into a formal procedure. Integration and coordination between different levels of management and functional areas should support firm violation enforcement provisions. These can include disciplinary and corrective actions to help reinforce established codes of practice throughout the organization.

The charts on the next page illustrate the above steps graphically.

Developing an Internal Control System

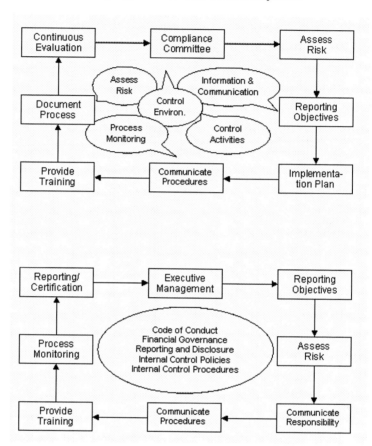

48

BUSINESS PROCESS CONTROLS

Sarbanes-Oxley requires top executives to confirm that their internal control structure is functioning effectively. This means they will need to be very attuned to the various business process controls and stay well informed. To accomplish this, they must establish a link between the control activities of the organization and the governance activities of the Board and executives. Sarbanes-Oxley requires a bottom-up approach to controls with line mangers along the way certifying (formally or informally) that the information received and passed on is complete and accurate.

This link will be facilitated by effective communication and this emphasis on communication will have broad-reaching effects on all aspects of business. Strong internal controls have long been flouted as necessary best practice, but unfortunately, their implementation was often nixed by cost benefit analysis. Now, Sarbanes-Oxley provides a strong impetus to revive those internal control plans and the bonus will be greater chance of business success. Company Management is responsible for creating and maintaining thorough internal control structures and identifying how effective the internal control structure and financial reporting procedures are (at the end of the most recent fiscal year). The company's auditor is required to confirm the validity of the internal control report.

INFORMATION TECHNOLOGY CONTROLS

Management must first set the criteria for scope decisions (i.e. financial reporting elements, process documentation, and the depth of management's assessment of controls design and effectiveness):

- Define documentation and assessment methodology to support assertions on internal control, and provide a basis for the independent public accountant to review and test.

- Break down the organization to evaluate entity-level and process-level controls.
- Identify the technology and tools needed to support the controls evaluation process. The method should be robust, to ensure enterprise-wide consistencies.
- Agree to and validate an approach with external, independent public accountants to ensure all concur.
- Define and distribute a communications plan during the project.

Control Processes - IT and Process Owners

Control processes address multiple objectives:

- Financial Reporting
- Regulatory Compliance
- Internal Operations

Management is not required to evaluate internal controls over operations, except to the extent that operational control overlaps with financial and regulatory compliance issues. By defining, documenting and implementing operational procedures, these controls are more often related to financial reporting activities. Also, some compliance controls may be connected to SEC rules and regulations (impact assessment of changes, articulating reporting policies and communicating such policies throughout the organization).

Process owners must document and communicate policies and procedures regarding IT, managed by control owners and other assigned personnel. Relevant and reliable information is necessary to understand and control external and internal business processes. Performance measures regarding communication processes are essential to proper internal control within the process. IT and the process owner must be responsible for:

- Access control over sensitive and critical applications and data files supporting the process (including security for preventing viruses and hacker intrusion).

- Authorization, documentation, testing and organizing the implementation of new applications that have an impact on the process.
- Backup and recovery procedures for all critical applications and data files supporting the process.
- Being committed to assurance that all pertinent information is captured close to sources, accurately recorded and processed, and promptly reported for analysis, evaluation and use in financial reports.
- Capturing adequate information—with full executive management support—from external sources to assess the impact on the process by external environmental changes, impacts on performance and the information about that performance (i.e., customer needs and desires, competitive, technological and regulatory issues, and general economic and industry trends and conditions).
- Having access to information about changing conditions and trends affecting the performance of the process.
- Ensuring relevant information is provided on a timely basis, to control owners and other process personnel in detail to enable them to carry out responsibilities.
- Communicating process objective to control owners and other process personnel; facilitate communications within the process and the realm of stakeholders; and support a process for control owners and other personnel to convey upward issues regarding process performance and control.

ASSESSING INTERNAL CONTROL

Management and the CEO and CFO must perform an internal control evaluation and prepare a report attesting to the effectiveness of the controls as of the end of the fiscal year. Material changes in the internal control system must be reported during the fiscal quarter it occurred if it is likely to affect financial reports. The report must address the design and the effectiveness of the system and management must demonstrate they performed actual tests on the controls. It is important to note that the system's effectiveness needs to be confirmed; a "negative assurance" or statement that "nothing has come to management's attention" is not sufficient.

Although the SEC has not prescribed any one method of evaluating internal control, it does require that a suitable, recognized framework be used. For a framework to be suitable, it must be free from bias, be qualitatively and quantitatively consistent, be sufficiently complete, and be relevant. The most common and most recommended system is COSO (some advocate for it to be the mandated system) and the five criteria used and recommended by COSO to assess the reliability are:

- Extent of Documentation
- Awareness of System (communication)
- Monitoring
- Design Effectiveness
- Operating Effectiveness

Placing the 5 components of internal control along the top and the elements of reliability on the side, the following grid can be used to assess the reliability of the entire control system.

	Control Environment	Risk Assessment	Control Activities	Information, Communication	Monitoring
Extent of Documentation					
Awareness of System/ Communication					
Monitoring					
Design Effectiveness					
Operating Effectiveness					

Design effectiveness refers to whether a control is able to prevent or detect material inaccuracies in specific financial statement report items. It involves consideration of the financial reporting objectives that the control is meant to achieve. Operating effectiveness refers to whether the control is functioning properly and as intended. During the evaluation of operating effectiveness, management gathers evidence regarding how the control was applied, the consistency with which it was applied, and who applied it.

CHAPTER 3
CONTROL ENVIRONMENT

The control environment is the control consciousness of an organization; it is the atmosphere in which people conduct their activities and carry out their control responsibilities. An effective control environment is an environment where competent people understand their responsibilities, the limits to their authority, and are knowledgeable, mindful, and committed to doing what is right and doing it the right way; they are committed to following an organization's policies and procedures and its ethical and behavioral standards. The control environment encompasses technical competence and ethical commitment; it is an intangible factor that is essential to effective internal control.

It is necessary to evaluate the entire organizational environment to determine if broad based controls are working and are being observed. Management may evaluate the design of a code of conduct by considering whether the code is comprehensive and detailed enough to guide ethical decisions. It may verify that the code of conduct is sent to all personnel and that all personnel sign-off on such policies. This is one way to ascertain that the code is actually contributing to compliance and allows management to evaluate the operating effectiveness of this control. Another example may be to consider if job descriptions are adequately designed to include all relevant tasks of a position in sufficient detail. Determining if employees are aware of the job descriptions, participate in updates to them, and adhere to the descriptions may provide evidence of their operating effectiveness.

RISK ASSESSMENT

Risk assessment is the identification and analysis of risks associated with the achievement of operations, financial reporting, and compliance goals and objectives. This, in turn, forms a basis for determining how those risks should be managed. Risk assessment is one of management's responsibilities and enables management to act proactively in reducing unwanted surprises. Failure to consciously manage these risks can result in a lack of confidence that operation, financial and compliance goals will be achieved.

A risk is anything that could jeopardize the achievement of an objective. Asking the following questions helps to identify risks:

- What could go wrong?
- How could we fail?
- What must go right for us to succeed?
- Where are we vulnerable?
- What assets do we need to protect?
- Do we have liquid assets or assets with alternative uses?
- How could someone steal from the department?
- How could someone disrupt our operations?
- How do we know whether we are achieving our objectives?
- On what information do we most rely?
- On what do we spend the most money?
- How do we bill and collect our revenue?
- What decisions require the most judgment?
- What activities are most complex?
- What activities are regulated?
- What is our greatest legal exposure?

It is important that risk identification be comprehensive, both at the department level and at the activity or process level, for operations, financial reporting, and compliance objectives, considering both external and internal risk factors.

Usually, several risks can be identified for each objective. Management may consider if its risk assessment includes the effects of intense competitive pressures on revenue recognition practices. In evaluating the design of the risk assessment process, management may consider the thoroughness of procedures to identify business units experiencing competitive pressures and the likelihood of inappropriate revenue recognition practices occurring as a result, whether accounting personnel are involved in the risk assessment, and whether there are procedures for implementing follow-up control activities or monitoring.

Inspecting risk assessments to determine whether relevant risks were identified and inquiry of personnel to determine the appropriateness of follow-up actions may provide the basis for an evaluation of operating effectiveness. Management may review the policies and procedures that articulate when and how often information technology (IT) risk assessments are required and the program of risk assessments planned. Operating effectiveness may be evaluated by examining the results of risk assessments performed, conclusions reached, and documentation of activities to mitigate risks.

Control Activities

Control activities are actions supported by policies and procedures that, when carried out properly and in a timely manner, manage or reduce risks. Controls can be either preventive or detective. The intent of these controls is different. Preventive controls attempt to deter or prevent undesirable events from occurring. They are proactive controls that help to prevent a loss. Examples of preventive controls are separation of duties, proper authorization, adequate documentation, and physical control over assets.

Detective controls, on the other hand, attempt to detect undesirable acts. They provide evidence that a loss has occurred but do not prevent a loss from occurring. Examples of detective controls are reviews, analyses, variance analyses, reconciliations, physical inventories, and audits. Both types of controls are essential to an effective internal control system. From a quality standpoint, preventive controls are essential because they are proactive and emphasize quality. However, detective controls play a critical role in providing evidence that the preventive controls are functioning and preventing losses.

Control activities include approvals, authorizations, verifications, reconciliations, reviews of performance, security of assets, segregation of duties, and controls over information systems and are further explained as follows:

- **Approvals, Authorizations, and Verifications (Preventive):** Management authorizes employees to perform certain activities and to execute certain transactions within limited parameters. In addition, management specifies those activities or transactions that need supervisory approval before they are performed or executed by employees. A supervisor's approval (manual or electronic) implies that he or she has verified and validated that the activity or transaction conforms to established policies and procedures.
- **Reconciliations (Detective):** Employees relate different sets of data to one another, identify and investigate differences, and take corrective action when necessary.
- **Reviews of Performance (Detective):** Management compares information about current performance to budgets, forecasts, prior periods, competitors, or other benchmarks to measure the extent to which goals and objectives are being achieved and to identify unexpected results or unusual conditions that require follow-up.
- **Security of Assets (Preventive and Detective):** Access to equipment, inventories, securities, cash and other assets is restricted; assets are periodically counted and compared to amounts shown on control records.
- **Segregation of Duties (Preventive):** Duties are segregated among different people to reduce the risk of error or inappropriate action. Normally, responsibilities for authorizing transactions, recording transactions (accounting), and handling the related asset (custody) are divided.
- **Controls Over Information Systems (Preventive and Detective):** Controls over information systems are grouped into two broad categories- general controls and application controls. General controls commonly include controls over data

center operations, system software acquisition and maintenance, access security, and application system development and maintenance. Application controls, such as computer matching and edit checks, are programmed steps within application software; they are designed to help ensure the completeness and accuracy of transaction processing, authorization, and validity. General controls are needed to support the functioning of application controls; both are needed to ensure complete and accurate information processing.

Control activities must be implemented thoughtfully, conscientiously, and consistently; a procedure will not be useful if performed mechanically without a sharp continuing focus on the conditions to which the policy is directed. Further, it is essential that unusual conditions identified as a result of performing control activities are investigated and appropriate corrective action is taken. Management may consider the design of online authorizations for purchases and whether all types and values of purchases are included in the authorization. Operating effectiveness may be evaluated by queries of authorization tables in the system. The evaluation may include consideration of general controls such as system access and program change controls. Management may consider the design of segregation of duties between personnel who deposit cash receipts and those who prepare bank reconciliations. Operating effectiveness may be evaluated by inspecting signatures indicating which personnel deposit cash receipts and which prepare bank reconciliations.

Information and Communication

Information and communication are essential to effecting control; information about an organization's plans, control environment, risks, control activities, and performance must be communicated up, down, and across an organization. Reliable and relevant information from both internal and external sources must be identified, captured, processed, and communicated to the people who need it, in a form and timeframe that is useful. Information systems produce reports containing operational, financial, and compliance-related information that makes it possible to run and control an organization.

Information and communication systems can be formal or informal. Formal information and communication systems, which range from sophisticated computer technology to simple staff meetings, should provide input and feedback data relative to operations, financial reporting, and compliance objectives; such systems are vital to an organization's success. Just the same, informal conversations with customers, suppliers, regulators, and employees often provide some of the most critical information needed to identify risks and opportunities. When assessing internal control over a significant activity (or process), the key questions to ask about information and communication are as follows:

- Do departments get the information they need from internal and external sources in a form and time frame that is useful?
- Do departments get information that alerts them to internal or external risks (e.g. legislative, regulatory, and developmental)?
- Do departments get information that measures their performance; information that tells the department whether it is achieving its operations, financial reporting, and compliance objectives?
- Do departments identify, capture, process, and communicate the information that others need (e.g. information used by our customers or other departments) in a form and time frame that is useful?
- Do departments provide information to others that alerts them to internal or external risks?
- Do departments communicate effectively, both internally and externally?

Information and communication are simple concepts. Nevertheless, communicating with and getting information to people in a form and time frame that is useful to them is a constant challenge. Management may consider the design of procedures for involvement of the accounting department in changes to a company's enterprise resource planning (ERP) system, including sign-offs on changes.

Operating effectiveness may include inquiry as to whether the accounting department's involvement actually occurred and the level of the involvement reported, and inspection of evidence such as signoffs or project plans indicating the personnel involved. A typical class of transactions a company may process is payroll, which involves the capture of payroll changes and the recording of payroll liabilities in the general ledger. Management may consider whether the design of the process ensures that the right information is provided in sufficient detail and on a timely basis to ensure payroll liabilities are complete and accurate, including, for example, vacation accruals.

Evaluation of operating effectiveness may be performed by inquiry of personnel about the timeliness and accuracy of the information received and by inspecting payroll and accounting records. Management may consider the design of decision processes related to business expansions, acquisitions, and contractions and the extent to which timely and relevant information is passed to the tax department for consideration of tax applicability. Operating effectiveness may be evaluated by reviewing meeting minutes or other documentation as evidence of the required participation, information flow, and analysis.

CHAPTER 4
MONITORING

Monitoring is the assessment of internal control performance over time; it is accomplished by ongoing monitoring activities and by separate evaluations of internal controls such as self-assessments, peer reviews, and internal audits. The purpose of monitoring is to determine whether internal controls are adequately designed, properly executed, and effective. Internal controls are adequately designed and properly executed if all five internal control components (Control Environment, Risk Assessment, Control Activities, Information and Communication, and Monitoring) are present and functioning as designed. Internal controls are effective if the Board of Trustees and management have reasonable assurance that:

- They understand the extent to which operations objectives are being achieved.
- Published financial statements are being prepared reliably.
- Applicable laws and regulations are being compiled.
- While internal control is a process, its effectiveness is an assessment of the condition of the process at one or more points in time.

Just as control activities help to ensure that actions to manage risks are carried out, monitoring helps to ensure that control activities and other planned actions to effect internal control are carried out properly and in a timely manner and that the end result is effective internal control. Ongoing monitoring activities include various management and supervisory activities that evaluate and improve the design, execution, and effectiveness of internal control. Separate evaluations, on the other hand, such as self-assessments and internal audits, are periodic evaluations of internal control components, resulting in a formal report on internal control. Department employees perform self-assessments; internal auditors provide an independent appraisal of internal control perform internal audits.

Management's role in the internal control system is critical to its effectiveness. Managers, like auditors, don't have to look at every single piece of information to determine that the controls are functioning and should focus their monitoring activities on high-risk areas. The use of spot checks of transactions or basic sampling techniques can provide a reasonable level of confidence that the controls are functioning. Operating effectiveness may be evaluated by considering instances of follow-up action when tolerances were exceeded, the level of tolerances used, and frequency of the analysis. In evaluating design, management may consider whether deficiencies have been identified and the nature of those deficiencies. To evaluate operating effectiveness, management may review supporting documentation indicating evidence of follow-up and corrective action, such as changes in policy, to correct control deficiencies.

CHAPTER 5
MATERIAL WEAKNESSES

The SEC, relying on Auditing Standards No. 60, states that a control system, or part thereof, is judged ineffective if there are any "material weakness," where material weakness is defined as "a reportable condition in which the design or operation of one or more of the internal control components does not reduce to a relatively low level, the risk that misstatements caused by errors or fraud in amounts that would be material in relation to the financial statements being audited may occur and not be detected within a timely period by employees in the normal course of performing their assigned functions." Any material weakness must be reported in the management report on internal control. The SEC has further stated that an aggregation of reportable conditions could constitute a material weakness.

SPECIFIC INTERNAL CONTROLS TO EVALUATE

The SEC has suggested certain types of controls that should be included in the evaluation process, including, but not limited, to:

- Initiating, recording, processing, and reconciling account balances
- Classes of transactions and disclosure-related assertions contained in the financial statements
- Initiating and processing of non-routine and non-systematic transactions
- Selection and application of accounting policies
- Prevention, identification and detection of fraud

DISCLOSURE COMMITTEE

The SEC has recommended that companies create a disclosure committee to consider significance of information, disclosure requirements, identify relevant disclosure issues and coordinate the development of infrastructure. The disclosure committee would report to and include senior management, specifically the certifying officers. When certifying officers sign certifications, they are representing that they possess or have access to the collective knowledge of the company regarding all information that is significant to investors. They are also certifying management's internal processes; therefore, control over financial reporting is integral to the certification process. Important activities for the Disclosure Committee include:

- Ensure disclosure guidelines are in place.
- Make sure to identify and disclose that the company is compliant with legal and regulatory requirements.
- Set an appointment to meet alone with the Audit Committee at least twice each year.
- Set up a verification of work plans with auditors, and then seek approval of plans from the CEO and Audit Committee.
- Ensure that a documenting system is in place that will allow the corporation to meet the requirement of disclosing any changes in finances or operations within the required two-business-day timeframe.
- Establish how frequently controls will need self-assessment to ensure continued compliance with the Act.
- Find out what the external auditor requires and expects from internal control documentation.
- Determine how the external auditor plans to measure the level of effectiveness of internal controls.
- Create both a positive and non-threatening disclosure atmosphere by frequently communicating what the disclosure expectations are.

A Proposed Auditing Standard

On October 7, 2003, the PCAOB put forth a proposed standard on the Audit of Internal Control Over Financial Reporting Performed in Conjunction with an Audit of Financial Statements. The Board is receiving feedback on the proposal for 45 days and a ruling will be issued accordingly. A proposed standard will go a long way to assist companies in their compliance efforts, as it will provide a solid framework to structure their audits. The proposed standard includes the following:

- The proposed standard refers to an internal control audit rather than an attestation and it specifies that it is to be performed in conjunction with a financial statement audit.
- The proposed standard is based on the evaluation of "management's assessment of internal controls." This means that the auditors must satisfy themselves that management has an evaluation process in place and whether that process yields accurate results. Even though the auditor is using management's assessment as its guide, it is understood that the Auditor may perform actual tests of the system.
- The proposed standard provides a specific framework to determine the significance of a deficiency and it provides examples on how to apply the framework.
- The proposed standard addresses the issue of cost of the internal control assessment versus the benefit of it. It also recognizes that a one-size-fits-all standard is not necessarily appropriate, given the resource and economic disparities between large corporations and small to mid-sized ones.
- The proposed standard indicates the rotation process that auditors should apply when auditing the corporation from year to year.
- The proposed standard requires auditors to follow a significant process from its original recording through to the financial statement.

If accepted, this standard will be extremely useful for corporations and will set an equal playing field for all companies to assess themselves.

The Limits of Internal Control

Because control systems are designed and built by humans, they have human fallibility and internal control can always be circumvented by fraudulent abuse, decreased through carelessness, and eliminated through resource constraints. The benefits of internal control needs to be continuously monitored and the processes changed to maintain effectiveness and diligence.

Remember: Internal control can help to mitigate risks but it does not eliminate it.

CHAPTER 6
IMPLEMENTING SARBANES-OXLEY

WHAT DOES COMPLIANCE LOOK LIKE?

TimeLine
(Subject to change since time of first writing)

Sec	Provision	Status as of August 2003 (Please review current documentation at www.SarbanesOxleyGuide.com for latest timelines and worksheets).
101	PCAOB Recognition	Effective for annual filings for the first fiscal year ending after December 15, 2003
201	Non-Audit Services	Adopted January 28, 2003, but services that were contracted before May 6, 2003 are allowed so long as they are completed by May 6, 2004.
301	Audit Committee – Independent Director and Responsibilities	Compliance is required by the earlier of the first annual meeting after January 15, 2004 or October 31, 2004.
302	CEO/CFO Certification	Effective for all reports due on or after August 14, 2003
906	CEO/CFO Certification	Effective for all reports due on or after August 14, 2003
304	Forfeiture of Bonuses and Profits	Effective July 30, 2002
306	Black-out Periods	Effective January 26, 2003
401	Off Balance Sheet Disclosures	Off Balance Sheet disclosures required on statements for fiscal years ending on or after July 15, 2003.

		Contractual Obligation disclosure is required on statements for fiscal years ending on or after December 15.
402	Prohibition of Loans to Executive	Effective July 30, 2002
403	Disclosure Of Insider Trades	Effective January 26, 2003
404	Internal Control Report	Accelerated filers are required to include the annual report for the first fiscal period ending on or after June 15, 2004. All others are required to include the annual report for the first fiscal period ending on or after April 15, 2005.
406	Code of Ethics	Required disclosure (or waiver of requirement) in annual reports for fiscal years ending on or after July 15, 2003.
407	Financial Expert on Audit Committee	Required compliance for annual reports with fiscal periods ending on or after July 15, 2003 (December 15, 2003 for small business).
409	Real-Time Disclosure	The SEC is not required to adopt specific rules.
806	Whistleblower Program	New civil and felony provisions are in place as of July 30, 2002.

Checklists

Audit Committee Compliance (Addresses Section 301)

- Confirm the external auditor has registered with the PCAOB (latest date for US Firms is Oct 22, 2003, Non US Firms is April 19, 2004).

70

- Set up a periodic confirmation that external auditor complies, and is in good standing with the PCAOB.
- Establish a Charter for the Audit Committee (may be a separate committee from the Board of Directors), and ensure that the committee is responsible for reviewing:
  o Critical accounting practices
  o Alternative treatments of financial information under GAAP
  o Material communication between the Auditor and Management
- Ensure that the Audit Committee is composed of independent board members as defined by the SEC.
- Arrange for a Financial Expert (as defined by the SEC) to be on the Committee.
- Ensure the Audit Committee is responsible for approving all non-audit services provided by the audit firm and has set procedures in place to do so.
- Rotate the lead of the audit partner every five years.
- Prohibit hiring of employees from the audit firm for 12 months after they leave their position, and have the audit firm prohibit hiring employees from the Corporation for 12 months after that employee leaves the Corporation.
- Establish procedures for the Audit Committee to evaluate all practices of Management and the Board to ensure integrity and ethical behavior.
- Establish procedures to deal with Forfeiture of Bonuses and Profits or other sanctions required for noncompliance.
- Develop a procedure to respond to employee concerns.
- Meet with the CFO and the Auditors separately at least twice a year.

- Ensure that management evaluates business risks and internal control systems at least once a year, and conduct a separate review of management's assessment process.
- Evaluate trades occurring during blackout periods to ensure compliance with the Act.
- Keep current on all regulatory and governance issues that impact the Corporation and the Board.

Compliance Committee (Addresses section 302 CEO/CFO Certification)

- Ensure the CFO is on the committee and include the CEO, CIO, and other key executives (HR, Legal, Operations, Sales, etc...) where possible.
- Asses and document identified risks.
- Establish objectives.
- Confirm that all polices and procedures comply with the Act and are reasonable given industry norms. Communicate and enforce these policies and procedures.
- Provide training where necessary to ensure understanding.
- Draft and communicate policies related to:
    - Financial Statement preparation
    - Involvement of Internal Auditors with the External Auditor
    - Off Balance Sheet transactions
    - Evaluation of Internal control systems
    - Code of Ethics
    - Moving toward "real-time" disclosure
- Establish procedures to disclose material changes in financial positions or operations within two business days.
- Ensure that the company website addresses material changes within the disclosure time frame.

72

- Reevaluate key performance indicators to ensure they are reasonable and attainable within an ethical and transparent work environment.
- Address and implement all audit recommendations.
- Establish a Whistle Blower program and communicate details of program and employee protection.
- Document all processes and internal control systems.
- Manage the change process through open communication and fair practice.
- Consider hiring an external party to assess the above activities.

Internal Control Report (Addresses section 404)

- Ensure the Compliance Committee understands their roles and responsibilities.
- Ensure the Compliance committee consistently applies no-tolerance to any activity that is not in compliance with the Act.
- Review the compliance efforts for appropriateness and completeness.
- Ensure that the definitions of "independent" and "financial-expert" have been met.
- Ensure the compliance plan and all processes have been documented.
- Ensure the documentation is standardized across the corporation.
- Ensure the documentation is easily accessible and current.
- Establish a process to monitor operations, the environment, and ensure continuous improvement.
- Test your ability to meet the disclosure deadlines (i.e. simulate a material event and ensure disclosure within two business days).
- Monitor the effectiveness of the Compliance Committee:
  - Is there a charter and agenda?
  - Are the committee members satisfied with their roles and progress?
  - Has the Committee's purpose been effectively communicated?
- Satisfy that all elements of the "Certification" for Internal and Disclosure controls can be attested to. See below for Certification documents prescribed by the SEC.

You will find the following certifications and other useful information at the SEC's Web Site:

http://www.sec.gov/rules/proposed/33-8212.htm

For soft-copies of these forms, please visit www.SarbanesOxleyGuide.com.

CERTIFICATION (internal controls)

I, [identify the certifying individual], certify that:

1. I have reviewed this annual report on Form 20-F of [identify registrant];

2. Based on my knowledge, this report does not contain any untrue statement of a material fact or omit to state a material fact necessary to make the statements made, in light of the circumstances under which such statements were made, not misleading with respect to the period covered by this report;

3. Based on my knowledge, the financial statements, and other financial information included in this report, fairly present in all material respects the financial condition, results of operations and cash flows of the registrant as of, and for, the periods presented in this report;

4. The registrant's other certifying officers and I are responsible for establishing and maintaining disclosure controls and procedures (as defined in Exchange Act Rules 13a-15 and 15d-15) for the registrant and have:

(a) Designed such disclosure controls and procedures to ensure that material information relating to the registrant, including its consolidated subsidiaries, is made known to us by others within those entities, particularly during the period in which this report is being prepared;

(b) Evaluated the effectiveness of the registrant's disclosure controls and procedures as of a date within 90 days prior to the filing date of this report (the "Evaluation Date"); and

(c) Presented in this report our conclusions about the effectiveness of the disclosure controls and procedures based on our evaluation as of the Evaluation Date;

5. The registrant's other certifying officers and I have disclosed, based on our most recent evaluation, to the registrant's auditors and the audit committee of registrant's board of directors (or persons performing the equivalent functions):

(a) All significant deficiencies in the design or operation of internal controls which could adversely affect the registrant's ability to record, process, summarize and report

financial data and have identified for the registrant's auditors any material weaknesses in internal controls; and
(b) Any fraud, whether or not material, that involves management or other employees who have a significant role in the registrant's internal controls; and
6. The registrant's other certifying officers and I have indicated in this report whether there were significant changes in internal controls or in other factors that could significantly affect internal controls subsequent to the date of our most recent evaluation, including any corrective actions with regard to significant deficiencies and material weaknesses.
* Provide a separate certification for each principal executive officer and principal financial officer of the registrant.

Date: ....   [Signature]
Place: ....   [Title]

CERTIFICATIONS (disclosure controls)

I, [identify the certifying individual], certify that:

1. I have reviewed this annual report on Form 40-F of [identify registrant];

2. Based on my knowledge, this report does not contain any untrue statement of a material fact or omit to state a material fact necessary to make the statements made, in light of the circumstances under which such statements were made, not misleading with respect to the period covered by this report;

3. Based on my knowledge, the financial statements, and other financial information included in this report, fairly present in all material respects the financial condition, results of operations and cash flows of the registrant as of, and for, the periods presented in this report;

4. The registrant's other certifying officers and I are responsible for establishing and maintaining disclosure controls and procedures (as defined in Exchange Act Rules 13a-15 and 15d-15) for the registrant and have:

(a) Designed such disclosure controls and procedures to ensure that material information relating to the registrant, including its consolidated subsidiaries, is made known to us by others within those entities, particularly during the period in which this report is being prepared;

(b) Evaluated the effectiveness of the registrant's disclosure controls and procedures as of a date within 90 days prior to the filing date of this report (the "Evaluation Date"); and

(c) Presented in this report our conclusions about the effectiveness of the disclosure controls and procedures based on our evaluation as of the Evaluation Date;

5. The registrant's other certifying officers and I have disclosed, based on our most recent evaluation, to the registrant's auditors and the audit committee of registrant's board of directors (or persons performing the equivalent functions):

(a) All significant deficiencies in the design or operation of internal controls which could adversely affect the registrant's ability to record, process, summarize and report financial data and have identified for the registrant's auditors any material weaknesses in internal controls; and

(b) Any fraud, whether or not material, that involves management or other employees who have a significant role in the registrant's internal controls; and

6. The registrant's other certifying officers and I have indicated in this report whether there were significant changes in internal controls or in other factors that could significantly affect internal controls subsequent to the date of our most recent evaluation, including any corrective actions with regard to significant deficiencies and material weaknesses.

* Provide a separate certification for each principal executive officer and principal financial officer of the registrant.

Date: ....   [Signature]
Place: ....   [Title]

Build an Effective Whistleblower Program

"Approximately one third of American employees have witnessed unethical or illegal conduct in their workplace. Of these, over half did not disclose what they observed."
Dawson, 2000

"71 percent of respondents expected that people who reported corruption would suffer for reporting it."
Zipparo, 1999

Section 301 of the Sarbanes-Oxley Act requires Audit Committees to establish procedures for receiving and handling complaints related to "accounting, internal accounting controls, or auditing matters; and the confidential, anonymous submission by employees of the issuer of concerns regarding questionable accounting or auditing matters." Effective whistleblower programs will help organizations meet these requirements.

Factors that Contribute to Employee Disclosures

Protection
Employees are usually reluctant to blow the whistle for fear of retaliation, including discrimination, harassment, intimidation, alienation, targeted supervision and in some cases even termination. Reassurance that management will protect whistleblowers from retaliation and that legal safeguards are in place, will help to create an environment where employees feel that disclosing their concerns is acceptable and encouraged.

Accessibility
Making the disclosure must be easy and convenient, preferably with a few different options for the employee to choose from.

Tone at the Top
A management team that sends a clear and consistent message to behave ethically, with integrity, fairness, openness, and compliance with the law will foster

a workforce that will police itself. The corporate culture will support intolerance of fraudulent or inappropriate behavior and employees will expect that from their coworkers and supervisors.

Awareness

Awareness and acceptance of the whistleblower program, the rationale for its existence, and management's support will create an environment where employees know immediately what to do if they ever encounter a questionable situation.

Steps for Building Effective Whistleblower Programs - Development Stages

Assessment

- Assess employee characteristics and the needs of the organization.
- Ensure that all locations across the country or worldwide have access to the program.
- Ensure that the program operators can deliver support in any of the languages needed.
- Access to the program should be free (or very inexpensive), uncomplicated, and anonymous where possible. A toll-free number, fax access, e-mail, or a program ombudsman are all options.
- Provide availability 24 hours a day, 7 days a week.
- Evaluate whether to in-source or outsource the program.
- Establish a protocol for the program staff to follow.
- Establish a committee to oversee the appropriate handling of disclosures.
- Provide a reasonable budget.

Design

- Build the program that addresses the corporation's needs as established above.

- Provide training for staff (if in-sourcing) and the committee that will oversee the program.
- Develop policies and procedures making the whistleblower program an official component of the organization's system of internal controls.

Implement

- Communicate the program effectively. The preferred method would be a face-to-face meeting with employees describing the program and its development. Other options include email, memo, video conferencing, or CBT (Computer Based Training) program.
- Release the program throughout the organization at the same time.

Evaluate

- Conduct surveys to obtain feedback and make sure that employees remain aware that the program is in place and working effectively.
- Use the committee to gather statistics of use, effectiveness, and outcomes.
- Keep audit Committee apprised of the program.
- Keep the program visible. Mention it at staff meetings, in newsletters, on bulletin boards, etc.

REPORTING, DOCUMENTATION, AND ARCHIVING

Sarbanes-Oxley requires an unprecedented amount of relevant documentation, which must be accessible and easy to follow if and when an audit of the corporation's processes, systems, reports, or statements occurs. This demand presents a dilemma in that it will be important to maintain records, but only to the point where those records do not present a liability. The idea that all records should be kept forever is an extreme reaction and the possession of these records is a source of business risk.

Records management is a driver for a successful compliance effort. Emails, forms, reports, images, web content, and office documents are all records that need managing and are considered information assets. Policies and Procedures that outline how these records are to be stored and for how long will be very important to ensure compliance is maintained and also to ensure that incorrect information is not stored. Not only will policies and procedures have to be written to ensure standardized reporting, best practice will dictate a continuous documentation process with rules regarding how long information is to be kept and what type of information is to be archived or destroyed.

DISCLOSURE

As an effort to mandate transparent operations, Sarbanes-Oxley requires that many business activities be presented and explained to the public and stakeholders. Aside from reporting Internal Control Systems and Disclosure Controls and Procedures, compliance with the Act requires the following disclosures:

- Companies are required to disclose whether or not a financial expert serves on its auditing committee, disclose that person's name, and disclose if the person is independent.
- Public accounting firms must disclose whether or not they have a code of ethics for executive officers.
- All brokers, analysts, and securities analysts are required to disclose:
  - If they have any investments or debt with the company it is working with/reporting on.
  - If the compensation they are receiving is both beneficial to the public's interest and allows for protection of the investors.
  - If the issuer has been a client of the broker or dealer.

- o   If the analyst was compensated for any research reports based on investment banking revenues.
- Issuers must disclose, in understandable "plain" English, pertinent information, including quantitative and trends, regarding material changes in the issuer's financial situation or operations.
- Disclosures must be made in real time.
- All annual and quarterly reports must "disclose material off-balance sheet transactions, arrangements and obligations (this includes contingent obligations) in addition to other relationships the issuer has with unconsolidated entities and other individuals that may have an impact on material current or future effect on the issuer's financial condition, results of operations, liquidity, capital expenditures, capital resources or significant components of revenue or expenses."

CHAPTER 7
TECHNOLOGY IMPLICATIONS

Sections 302 and 404 require companies to evaluate the *effectiveness* of their internal controls over information reported to the financial markets. The SEC has issued rules to implement these statutory requirements and these will apply for financial year-ends on or after June 15, 2004 (for most companies) and on or after April 15, 2005 for others. This has a direct impact on the IT sector, the CIOs, CTOs and other IT professionals. Charged with analysis and design, systems development and maintenance responsibilities, IT professionals must be cognizant of the following:

- Turning compliance efforts from being just a tactical exercise into true, value-creating strategic IT initiatives.
- Enterprise Resource Planning (ERP) provides a foundation for compliance, performance, and quality.
- Systems based on spreadsheets are insufficient for the demands of Sarbanes-Oxley; procedures must be foolproof, automated, integrated and auditable.
- Compliance systems should have adequate virus and hacker security protection, backup schedules, backup restore testing, and documented disaster recovery plans.
- Business-critical processes should be resident on one platform.
- Real-time information must be accessible in case of problems, from anywhere, at anytime.
- Active enterprise-wide integration of all entities into defined policies, procedures, and processes.
- Application standards in target processes, day-to-day work, problem resolution, system controls, and risk management at all levels throughout the organization.

Section 404 Compliance has a definite impact on IT management in that processes are carried out by information systems, and systems are owned by IT. The first year of compliance will be the most costly, as companies use consultants and new technology to document and evaluate processes. But companies are positioning themselves to go forward on a self-sustaining basis. Most are not likely to hire new employees dedicated to Section 404 compliance.

Ideally, the key professional required in compliance system development is a Project Manager (PM) with a background in finance. Seasoned PMs are skilled and capable of matrix managing across multiple departments and timelines. Whether from internal audit, accounting, treasury or another finance area, the PM's expertise is most valuable. Internal audit, corporate and international finance experience is an advantage for the PM. The normal cycle for compliance systems development is depicted in the following illustration:

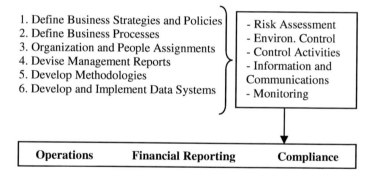

1. Define Business Strategies and Policies
2. Define Business Processes
3. Organization and People Assignments
4. Devise Management Reports
5. Develop Methodologies
6. Develop and Implement Data Systems

- Risk Assessment
- Environ. Control
- Control Activities
- Information and Communications
- Monitoring

| Operations | Financial Reporting | Compliance |

Compliance Systems Development

STORAGE SYSTEMS

Sarbanes-Oxley will have significant long-term effects on the storage industry. Analysis indicates a significant impact on enterprise storage environments and those who manage them:

- Scalability of storage subsystems will be required for compliance, especially large enterprises with high financial transaction volumes.
- The automatic capture and storage of financial data will be required.
- Compliance certification of storage infrastructure will be a critical factor.
- It will be difficult for organizations to extract data stored in unaltered form through changes in applications software, operating systems and storage devices.
- Communications between IT management and senior management will become more vital, policy-based, and will require more system resources.
- Compliance requirements, reporting requirements will force a tighter integration of mainframe and open systems and data stores.

IT SOLUTIONS

For most, the Section 404 solution will serve as a central repository for internal control documentation. It will also facilitate testing internal and external audit controls and serve as a portal for executive review. Like most rollouts, Section 404 software requires education in processes and internal controls.

Most products offered by vendors are Web-enabled, allowing clients with multiple locations to use the software with a minimum of IT staff. The use of XML, XBRL, JAVA and middleware languages is a success factor. Particularly in the case of XBRL, these languages bring the publication, exchange, and analysis of the complex financial information in corporate business reports into the interactive realm of the Internet.

XBRL provides a common platform for critical business reporting processes and improves the reliability and ease of communicating financial data among users internal and external to the reporting enterprise. XBRL is an XML-based, royalty-free, and open standard being developed by a consortium of over 170 companies and agencies, delivering benefits to investors, accountants, regulators, executives, business and financial analysts, and information providers.

Commercial packages typically include word processing, spreadsheets, diagramming and flowcharting tools to document processes and internal controls, which allows users to custom design software. Some solutions facilitate certification testing of controls by the business owner and the auditor. Others allow a view of best practices for internal controls, or the Committee of Sponsoring Organizations (COSO) Integrated Framework.

Various packages offer users the ability to resolve significant accounts from financial statements. Processes associated with selected accounts are identified and then assigned to process owners. Internal controls are documented and tested, and process owners can sign certifications for each process on a quarterly basis.

CHANGES IN IT MANAGEMENT

Complying with requirements of the Act represents a unique opportunity to pursue and implement best practices for planning, executing, reporting, and analyzing business performance. It is about both processes and systems; solid business rules, requirements, system specifications, development and documentation; proper implementation and enterprise wide training. At a minimum, the Software Development Life Cycle (SDLC) methodology must:

- Model the Processes
- Automate the Processes

88

- Manage and Monitor the Processes
- Analyze the Processes
- Integrate the Processes with relevant systems

The optimal methodology is to adopt CMM (Capability Maturity Model) practices. With the Year 2000 scare, the fact that companies searched software date bugs using a definite methodology forced them to clean up packages in the process. This also applies to the Act initiative; reporting systems will need to be more robust, have more integrity, be more flexible and be under tighter management controls over corporate destiny.

CHAPTER 8
SARBANES-OXLEY RELATED
BODIES

PCAOB

The Public Accounting Oversight Board (PCAOB) was established to ensure that covered individuals and entities fully comply with the Sarbanes-Oxley Act of 2002. The PCAOB is charged with setting audit firm standards and overseeing quality control, ethics, and independence issues. The board also has the power to discipline accountants. Implementing and enforcing the new standards will take time, perseverance and money. Currently funded by the government, it is a not-for-profit board that will levy fees on publicly-traded companies based on a corporation's size to sustain itself and companies with a market capitalization less than $25 million are exempt from the fees. The fees are not optional and some observers estimate that the largest companies could pay up to $1 million annually to support the PCAOB.

The Board consists of five members, appointed by the Securities and Exchange Commission, and must include a maximum of two CPAs. Members of the Board cannot be involved professionally in any other business activity and must be independent and full-time. The PCAOB will cooperate with advisory groups and professional accounting groups to help increase effectiveness of standards and setting standards. One of its main roles is to ensure auditor independence and it has not shied away from hotly contested issues like whether or not accounting firms should be allowed to participate in the lucrative business of performing tax services for an audit client. The following is a list of the PCAOB's activities:

- PCAOB registers public accounting firms.
- PCAOB is responsible for inspecting pubic accounting firms.
- PCAOB is responsible for investigating all claims and bringing forth disciplinary claims.

- It is mandatory that all domestic and foreign pubic accounting firms, who prepare/issue audit reports for any public company, register with the Board.
- If information pertaining to the registration application changes, companies must report that information.
- PCAOB can and may implement sanctions against registered accounting firms including: revoking a firm's registration, suspending or limiting its auditing activities or via censure or monetary penalties.

Although it was created with a very narrow scope of jurisdiction, namely the oversight of Sarbanes-Oxley, its mission is to create standards, register and inspect audit firms, and to discipline for audit problems as they relate to SEC registrants and their auditors. This means that the PCAOB's influence could extend to others who will undoubtedly look at what they do and believe that their standards and processes should be applied to private companies and other non-SEC registrants. Because the provisions of Sarbanes-Oxley are not necessarily relevant or applicable to non- SEC registrants, this has the potential to create a two-tiered system of auditing standards and peer review.

COSO

COSO is a voluntary organization that was formed in 1985 to sponsor the National Commission on Fraudulent Financial Reporting. Its mandate is to improve the quality of financial reporting through business ethics, effective internal controls, and corporate governance by studying the factors that lead to fraudulent reporting and developing recommendations to combat it. The Commission is backed by the American Accounting Association, the American Institute of Certified Public Accountants, the Financial Executives Institute, the Institute of Internal Auditors, and the National Association of Accountants (now the Institute of Management Accountants). The original Chairman of the National Commission was James C. Treadway, thus the popular name, "Treadway Commission" and the current chairman is John Flaherty, the retired Vice President and General Auditor for PepsiCo Inc.

COSO authored *Internal Control—Integrated Framework*, which set out a model for establishing and then evaluating internal control systems. Control activities centered on financial applications to protect integrity, confidentiality and availability, but they go beyond finance and address systems in all departments of an organization. This model is well respected, widely used, and has been loosely adopted by the SEC as an appropriate model for developing and evaluating internal control related to Sarbanes-Oxley. COSO developed its model and evaluation system based on four key concepts:

- Internal control is a process and as such is not static; it requires continuous assessment, evaluation, and modification.
- Internal control is more than written policies and procedures; it requires buy-in and acceptance from employees at all levels of the organization.
- Internal control does not guarantee results; it provides a reasonable assurance that the information is accurate but since the systems ultimately rely on human interaction or intervention, there is always room for error.
- Internal control is objective based; the objectives are achieved by controls in overlapping areas.

COSO has been very influential in the development and evolution of Sarbanes-Oxley. It's model has been proposed by the SEC as a standard for evaluating Internal Controls and it is looked upon as a leader in corporate governance issues.

SEC

The U.S. Securities and Exchange Commission (SEC) is set up to protect investors and maintain the integrity of the securities markets. Investing is risky and the public must have access to reliable information in order to make good decisions and protect their money to best of their ability. To ensure investors have access to this information, the SEC requires public companies to disclose meaningful financial and other information to the public. The SEC also oversees other investment organizations including stock exchanges, broker-dealers, investment advisors, mutual funds, and public utility holding companies. In order for the SEC to be effective, it has the authority to pass (per federal legislation) and enforce securities laws.

The SEC has adopted many of the provisions set out in the Sarbanes-Oxley Act and it oversees the PCAOB. Sarbanes-Oxley "requires the SEC to promulgate rules and regulations on the retention of any and all materials related to an audit, including communications, correspondence and other documents created, sent or received in connection with an audit or review." The following is a list of SEC authorities in addition to what has been discussed earlier:

- The SEC oversees the PCAOB.
- The SEC appoints the members of the board.
- The SEC can request a court order to bar a person from status as a director or an officer of an issuer if the person's behavior makes him unfit to serve in such a position.
- The SEC will review company filings at least once every three years.
- The SEC has provided a set of standards which attorneys must follow, including:
    o Any lawyer who works for a public company must report to the CEO or the chief counsel of the company if the lawyer has evidence of a securities violation or any violation by the company.
    o The lawyer then must ensure that the chief counsel or CEO takes action with the evidence. If they do not, the lawyer must advise the board of directors or audit committee of the evidence.

94

The SEC has been given a great deal of authority for rolling out the specifics of Sarbanes-Oxley and it is important to note that the SEC is susceptible to political pressures. Lawmakers have praised the SEC for its commitment to forwarding some of the most groundbreaking corporate reform since the 1930s. Advocates for investor groups, on the other hand, feel that the SEC softened almost all of the provisions in the Act in response to pressure from the accounting and legal professions. A particularly glaring example is the allowance by the SEC for Audit Committees to pre-approve non-audit services. Congress clearly wanted strict auditor independence, yet the SEC put in the pre-approval caveat to satisfy the protests of the accounting firms. It did, however, ban audit firms from providing financial-system implementation and internal audits. While the SEC has adopted many of the provisions of the Act, it is clear that the SEC has its own agenda and biases that it is working under.

FASB

The Financial Accounting Standards Board (FASB) was formed in 1973 to establish standards of financial accounting and reporting for private industry. While the SEC has statutory authority to establish these standards for publicly held companies, its policy is to rely on the private sector so long as it demonstrates the ability to function in the public's interest. To guarantee this public interest, the FASB is independent of all other business and professional organizations. The FASB also participates in international activities in an effort to improve comparability and quality standards between statements issued internationally and those issued in the US. The budget for the FASB comes from public accounting firm's annual fees and it receives independent funding under Sarbanes-Oxley.

CHAPTER 9
OPPORTUNITIES CREATED BY SARBOX

JOB OPPORTUNITIES

The employment opportunities created by Sarbanes-Oxley compliance efforts will be centered on finance, IT, and auditing roles. Whether firms choose to supplement their internal staff or choose to outsource some of the compliance activity, there will be a surge in the need for experienced, qualified professionals to lead or implement the required change. The stringent requirements of the new act mean that high-level executives want more experts on their staffs to assure them that the compliance efforts are effective and that they are designed properly. Many companies are creating the new position of Chief Risk Officer. This position would be in charge of leading the compliance committee; putting less pressure on the CFO and CIO, enabling them to focus more on their staff's needs during the process. Where companies choose not to add to the executive, the CIO and CFO will have new or more complex job descriptions and greater pressures. This may lead to a reevaluation of their job description and compensation.

> **Wanted: Sarbanes-Oxley Compliance Manager**
> Public Company seeks Sarbanes-Oxley Compliance Manager. In this internal controls function, the qualified candidate will be responsible for ensuring ongoing compliance with Sarbanes-Oxley as related to different business units. Focus on adequacy of internal controls and developing recommendations for improvement. Degree in Accounting and Public Audit experience required. CPA or MBA a plus.

The need for public and corporate accountants is also expected to rise dramatically to meet the vigorous demands of Sarbanes-Oxley. The level of detail required by the internal and external auditors means that extra manpower is inevitable. The standards for these professionals will also be strictly enforced and there will likely be an increased focus on training and professional development. To uncover fraud on a more aggressive basis, forensic accounting is an area of growth and demand. Already 40 % the top 100 accounting firms in the United States have expanded their forensic/fraud services.

An interesting twist to the employment opportunities created by Sarbanes-Oxley is the reluctance many finance professionals have for serving as directors or members of audit committees since the Act's inception. Many retired accountants, financial consultants and CFO's are hesitant to accept the "honor" of being asked to sit on a Board for fear of the legal liabilities they face with respect to the strict new standards. Sarbanes-Oxley has placed a much greater level of responsibility and accountability on the Audit committee members and so it is imperative that all members assess their risk associated with their duties in that capacity. Lawyers are cautioning all potential board members to make sure that the Board carries sufficient Directors and Officers Liability insurance and that it has a completely independent counsel. It should be very apparent from this guide that Sarbanes-Oxley means business and it has significant bite; it is, therefore, prudent to thoroughly evaluate one's own liability in relation to potential corporate misconduct.

OUTSOURCING

Outsourcing is expected to increase in the IT field as companies look to service providers who concentrate on Sarbanes-Oxley reform. Rather than develop sophisticated internal systems, it may make economic sense to hand a large portion of record management over to an outside company. Rather than "reinvent the wheel," companies are likely to explore ways to use other people's technology to accomplish their objectives. The problem with increased outsourcing is the fact that the firm is losing some of its control.

With the focus on control systems, this is a risk factor that must be thoroughly assessed before a decision to outsource is made. The rules and regulations surrounding outsourced contracts will likely become very strict and will involve a coordination of internal control and external controls to ensure data integrity. As it is the CEO and CFO have to certify that statements are accurate and that internal controls are effective; the level of accountability and scrutiny between partner companies will increase tremendously.

GLOBAL IMPACT

Some provisions of Sarbanes-Oxley conflict with the laws of other countries and that could pose big problems for non-US companies listed on the New York Stock Exchange and other US markets. Noncompliance could result in delisting and those companies considering entry into an American Exchange may put it off. 30% of the NYSE is made up of non-US companies and the loss of even just a few would have a negative impact on the US and foreign economies; US investors would have less access to foreign companies and foreign companies would have less access to American capital.

While the chance of a major worldwide departure from US markets is quite low, German companies will have a very difficult time complying with Sarbanes-Oxley. Their supervisory boards must include employee representatives who will not be able to pass any test for independence. This was a major factor in Porsche's decision not to list in the United States. The other main problem foreign companies will have is the restriction on loans to corporate directors, as this conflicts with many countries' customs and practices. The SEC has relaxed a few restrictions for foreign issuers, but the sentiment of the majority is against allowing too many concessions. Japan and Germany want to see foreign exemptions and they don't think that their management structures and in-house controls should have to match US standards.

In fact, Sarbanes-Oxley does apply US norms and culture to foreign subsidiaries or business units of

American multinationals. This creates conflict among the countries and within international corporations:

- Sarbanes-Oxley creates a conflict between Japan's goals in the market, which are to expand power, market share, and size and the goals of the United States and the United Kingdom, which are to maximize shareholder's profits.

- Europeans, for the most part, met Sarbanes-Oxley with objections and proceeded to lobby for exemptions.

- The Finance Ministers of the European Union oppose the requirement that foreign public accounting firms must register with the PCAOB and further "called for the negotiation of a transatlantic mutual recognition agreement based on home country control."

- In a survey by LexisNexis, the majority of lawyers surveyed, 700 worldwide, admitted they are concerned about the impact of Sarbanes-Oxley on the legal profession. They believe clients will be fearful of being open with their lawyers.

- One in 10 lawyers, a considerably low number, believe the act will bring more honesty from corporate executives.

- U.S. lawyers fear they won't get the opportunity to work with lawyers abroad until those lawyers understand the Sarbanes-Oxley Act intimately.

- Six hundred foreign attorneys were surveyed, and, according to LexisNexis, most were "confused and uncertain of the effects of Sarbanes-Oxley and the SEC rules."

- According to the report, lawyers from foreign countries are concerned the Act will attempt to prevail over national regulatory authorities in their respective countries.

- Ultimately, foreign issuers will likely have to adapt to the new regulations if they want to maintain access to the rich US capital market; a sacrifice most will be willing to make.

FUTURE

Two of the big questions relating to Sarbanes-Oxley are:

1. Will it restore public's faith in pubic accounting firms?
2. Will it restore investor's faith in public corporations?

Obviously the hope is to answer "yes" on both counts. It is undeniable that the public lost faith in both institutions as a result of the enormous fraud perpetuated by some highly respected and regarded companies. While faith that the reforms will work is generally high, of the executives surveyed half said they believed it would take time to gain the public's trust again. This is as expected and the onus is on every employee of every public company and every accountant to govern themselves in accordance with the principles of honesty and integrity. No one thinks that Sarbanes-Oxley will be an instant fix. "The last 10 years dug a very, very deep hole," says Lynn E. Turner, an accounting professor at Colorado State University and former chief accountant for the SEC. "Usually you aren't able to crawl out of a hole overnight. It's a three- to five-year process."

Sarbanes-Oxley has already had some positive effects. Analyst reports usually recommended investors "sell" in 1% of the situations discussed, now that figure has increased to 20%. This is a strong indication of more independence and less collusion between interested parties. The percentage of shareholders winning proxy fights has also increased and more shareholders brought motions against excessive compensation increases at this years AGMs. While the costs of compliance are high, in comparison to the astronomical losses suffered in the fall of Enron they are quite insignificant. Many of the reforms are not legally required until well into 2004 and 2005, so the results of this revolutionary act will take a few years to be thoroughly assessed. Regardless, 81% of the CEOs of United States' fastest growing companies believe the costs of compliance will only grow in the coming years.

CHAPTER 10
SUMMARY FOR THE CFO

In a poll of senior executives conducted by a major consulting firm:

- 42% of them felt that Sarbanes-Oxley was a step in the right direction, but that compliance costs place an excess burden on companies.
- 33% felt that Sarbanes-Oxley is a start but it is not sufficient in and of itself.
- 15% felt it was pushed through too quickly without enough consideration.
- 9% felt that is was adequate to address the current accounting and reporting issues.
- 1% felt I would be more detrimental to the market than helpful.

It is not surprising that legislation as revolutionary as Sarbanes-Oxley produces such divergent opinions and it will take time to assess the actual outcome. About one-third of executives believe Sarbanes-Oxley will restore public confidence in the capital markets, while half think it will have no impact.

Regardless of the outcome, what is certain is that Sarbanes-Oxley will change the face of corporate governance in the United States forever. Some of what is already taking place includes:

- Management certifications are being integrated into routine business and financial reporting processes.
- An increase in CEO involvement in financial reporting processes
- An increased use of technology to in current systems or new systems that leverages the ability to analyze and identify potential and actual inaccuracies

- A reinforcement of a culture that supports accountability, responsibility, and financial and business integrity across all levels of the organizations
- Increased engagement with external auditors, including more extensive discussions about accounting, reporting, internal controls, and audit-related matters
- Policies, procedures and standards are being created or formalized to identify and address all potential violations of organizations' ethical, professional, or financial reporting values.
- . Increased commitment from management provides business information that has potential financial consequences in a timely manner.
- . Internal audit responsibilities are shifting more toward oversight of financial integrity, including greater emphasis on the evaluation of financial related internal controls and the reliability of financial systems.
- . Executive management is linking the effectiveness of its internal controls over financial reporting to its certification under Section 302 of the Act and many companies are working on complying with section 404 as a way to further support the certification process.
- . The parent company's management certification process and corporate governance principles are replicated and leveraged at the subsidiary level, including overseas subsidiaries.
- . Disclosure committees that include representation from all departments and relevant SBUs have been formed and they are meeting quarterly to discuss business events, transactions and/or conditions requiring disclosure in the quarterly and annual reports.

Yes, the costs of compliance may be hefty at first; but the inevitable outcomes are more accurate financial reporting and quicker access to pertinent information; two things that should certainly improve investor confidence at least a little bit. The compliance effort will not come without pain and stress and fumbling; and executives are under great pressure to understand and apply the Act and to maintain a corporate environment that continuously supports the tenets of it: Accurate, timely, and transparent information.

While Sarbanes-Oxley itself focuses on financial data and information, the fallout from the efforts to comply will make each corporation stronger, healthier, and cohesive. The operational overhaul that is required will bring together all the disparate departments, business units, and functions; forcing them to discover the value that each brings to the organization as a whole. This understanding and awareness of how all the pieces fit together is a rich source of growth potential that can spurn the organization to accomplish objectives and develop strategies never before explored. Reform as broad and revolutionary as Sarbanes-Oxley is expected to cause some hardship; after all, if there is no pain there is no gain. Fortunately, what corporations stand to gain at the end is definitely worth their initial pain.

Part Two

Sarbanes-Oxley
For The
IT Professional

CHAPTER 11
INTRODUCTION
FOR THE IT PROFESSIONAL

THE GOAL

The goal of this part of this guide is to help a CIO or other senior-level IT professional understand the process to follow, from a technology perspective, to assist the CEO and the CFO in making the organization Sarbanes-Oxley compliant. It is designed to help the IT professional:

- Understand the Key Issues involved in addressing Sarbanes-Oxley compliance
- Visualize the IT infrastructure from the holistic perspective of Enterprise Technology Ecosystem, specifically:
  o The key business processes of the enterprise
  o The interaction of the key business processes with each other
  o The flow of value across the enterprise
  o The flow of information across the enterprise
  o The ecosystem of business applications inhabiting the enterprise
  o The ecosystem of key technologies inhabiting the enterprise
  o Formulating a vision for the future of the Enterprise Technology Ecosystem aligned with the strategic goals of the enterprise
- Understand the contributions of the Key Enterprise Technologies in facilitating Sarbanes-Oxley compliance
- Follow a well-defined process to enable the IT professional to create a Sarbanes-Oxley Compliant Key Enterprise Technology (SOCKET™) team. This SOCKET team will liaison with the Sarbanes-Oxley Compliance Committee under the CCO (Chief

Compliance Officer) and will cover all aspects of the enterprise technologies relevant to Sarbanes-Oxley.

Basic Premises

- In many ways Sarbanes-Oxley is no different from "IT as usual" and all the things that IT will do to become Sarbanes-Oxley compliant are really things that they should have been doing anyway.
- Sarbanes-Oxley is an opportunity to get systems in place to streamline organizational processes as well as to simplify and streamline reporting mechanisms.
- 80% of the companies already have 80% of the technology they need in order to achieve Sarbanes-Oxley compliance.

110

CHAPTER 12
THE ISSUES

FROM SARBANES-OXLEY TO SOCKET

The impact of Sarbanes-Oxley on IT can be logically arrived at through the process of "ripple-effect" reasoning:

- Sarbanes-Oxley impacts the CEO and CFO directly, since they need to certify the authenticity and accuracy of certain financial and related documents.
- This, in turn, impacts the Corporate Finance, Governance and Knowledge Management Systems that support the CEO and the CFO in generating those documents.
- This, in turn, impacts the Technology Infrastructure that, to a large extent, encapsulates and automates the above systems.
- The design and operations of this Technology Infrastructure is the responsibility of the IT department, headed up by a CIO and/or CTO.

The above ripple effect of Sarbanes-Oxley on the CIO and his/her IT department will need to be examined through the various intermediate stages to obtain an insight into the exact nature of its impact. The following sections explore this.

THE IMPACT OF SARBANES-OXLEY ON THE ENTERPRISE, THE CEO AND THE CFO

The main impact on the CEO, the CFO and the Enterprise as a whole arises out of Section 302 and Section 404. Section 302 requires them to personally certify the authenticity, accuracy and reliability of the financial reports. Section 404 requires them to certify the status of the Internal Controls.

Further, Section 409 discusses issues of real-time disclosure of material events. There are now nearly 20 material events listed by the SEC. Also, if we adhere to the spirit of the Act as opposed to its letter, then it is clear that the Sarbanes-Oxley Act is trying to maximize the factual representation of all financial information about a public company that management is aware of (and/or should be aware of). This includes projections, forecasts and all events or trends that will impact the company in the short- or long-term.

In summary then the major impact of Sarbanes-Oxley on the CEO, the CFO and, in general, on the enterprise is in the following key areas:

1. Accelerated reporting requirements:
    a. Reporting deadlines for filing periodic reports will arrive earlier.
    b. Faster reporting of significant internal or external "events" affecting the business condition is required (Sec. 409).
    c. Insider trading is to be reported much faster.
2. Certification Requirement:
    a. Review, Accuracy and Authenticity certification of all company filings by the CEO and CFO (Sec. 302 and Sec. 404)
3. Internal Controls (Sec. 404):
    a. Internal controls must be effective and strong and they must be verified in the annual filings to the SEC.
    b. CEOs and CFOs must inform their Board if significant internal control deficiencies exist.
4. Record Keeping:
    a. Auditors must maintain all documents and records pertaining to the audit for 7 years (Sec. 103).
    b. Strong criminal penalties for altering, destroying or falsifying records are imposed.
5. Conflict of Interest:

         a.   Audit firms cannot provide services for financial information systems design or implementation (Sec. 201).

         b.   Independent Audit Committee is created.

6.   Communication:

         a.   Allows whistleblowers to communicate independently with the Audit Committee (Sec. 301).

THE IMPACT OF SARBANES-OXLEY ON THE CORPORATE MANAGEMENT SYSTEMS

The CEO and the CFO rely on the Corporate Financial, Governance and Knowledge Management Systems for obtaining the financial and related information and documents they require to fulfill the certification and other requirements of Sarbanes-Oxley described above. The implications of Sarbanes-Oxley for the Corporate Management Systems are analyzed from an "essence", "spirit" or "holistic" perspective as well as from a more "reductionist" perspective in this section.

In spirit, the Sarbanes-Oxley Act is aimed at providing accurate and more "real-time"[1] corporate performance information to the investor. The ideal is that all relevant information that the CEO and the CFO observe during the normal course of business and that could impact the financials of the company by changing the direction of its strategic or operational course should be disclosed to the investor. Further, it is also aimed at ensuring that all the important and significant information reaches the CEO, the CFO and the investors in real-time; that is, that no important information be tampered with, hidden or delayed.

Such implementation of real-time reporting to the investor would result in a situation where investors will effectively be able to participate in corporate decision-

---

[1] Real-time implies a pre-defined time interval. So the information should reach the investor within a prescribed time interval of the information being generated. The prescribed timeframe according to Sarbanes-Oxley differs for different kinds of information.

making by "voting" on important events through means of the stock market. Positive information would immediately result in making the stock prices go up and negative information, such as the possibility of losing a large client, would result in an immediate drop in the stock prices of the company. This is the "corporate democracy" through which the investors would be able to influence the decision making of the company in real-time. It would also ensure that the CEO has the confidence of the Board as well as of the majority of the investors.

Thus, the Sarbanes-Oxley Act has implications far beyond sending CEOs to jail and makes the theoretical or philosophical foundations of public companies and stock markets practical.

The precise impact of Sarbanes-Oxley on the Corporate Management Systems from a reductionist perspective can be analyzed as follows:

Accelerated Reporting Requirements

The accelerated reporting requirements mean that reporting has to be made faster, ensuring that all relevant data is consolidated in the reporting system quickly and reports are generated faster. This requires:

1. That mechanisms exist in the enterprise to "quickly"[2] assemble all relevant data and information in a centralized data repository[3].
2. This centralized data repository should then be connected to an information and analysis system where the corporate analysts will quickly be able to analyze, judge and create an analytical report about the effect of

---

[2] See definition of real-time. Here, it is recommended that "quickly" be understood to mean much less than the minimum "real-time" time-interval defined in the Sarbanes-Oxley Act, i.e. two-days.

[3] Or centrally accessible data-repository. This allows a distributed data architecture but a centralized access architecture - possibly through a centralized meta-data repository.

114

any new event or information on the strategy and operations of the enterprise.

3. A Report Distribution System or Document Management and Workflow System will disburse this to the CEO and the CFO within the prescribed time frame and allow them enough time to make their own final judgments about the situation.

4. Finally, a Public Information Distribution System should exist to quickly disburse this information, if deemed important by the CEO and the CFO, to the investors and other stakeholders or relevant authorities prescribed by Sarbanes-Oxley.

Certification Requirement

The various certification requirements of Sarbanes-Oxley place the following requirements on the Corporate Management Systems:

- An accurate Data Capture System and a Document Capture System to capture data and relevant information at the point of generation of the information.
- Secure data and document travel from the point of generation to the point of storage.
- Centralized Data Repository and Document Repository to securely store the relevant and prescribed data and document.
- Secure Data and Document Retrieval System with hierarchical access control.
- Data and Document Retention, Destruction and Management system based on the corporate Data and Document policies.

Internal Controls

The internal control requirements entail:

- Seamless integration of all systems through which the financially relevant data, information and documents travel.

- Security systems to implement hierarchical access control policies.
- Workflow Management Systems to implement the proper control for financially relevant business decisions to be made through the appropriate decision-making chain of command.
- Business Process Monitoring and Management Systems to implement and monitor the key business processes of the enterprise and provide control over them to top management.

Record Keeping

Record keeping requirements are prescribed for the auditors. The auditors will be required to maintain the relevant records for 7 years. It makes good business sense to internally replicate the auditor's records for the same period of time. This forces the following requirements on the Corporate Management System:

- A Records Management System that allows secure and long-term storage of important documents and provides for implementing document destruction and retention policies.

Communications

IT can fulfill the communications requirement by implementing a secure and anonymous communication system between potential whistleblowers (meaning all employees) and the Corporate Audit Committee. The system should be accessible conveniently and anonymously by all employees and it should reach the Audit Committee within a reasonable time frame. Further, the Audit Committee should be able to archive all the complaints securely and be able to investigate and provide status reports on the investigations through that system. Also, once the investigation is closed and the final report is deposited, it should be stored securely and for the long-term.

116

THE IMPACT OF SARBANES-OXLEY ON THE TECHNOLOGY INFRASTRUCTURE

Most of the Corporate Management Systems listed above are encapsulated and implemented in Enterprise Applications and Technologies[4]. Crucial requirements of the Sarbanes-Oxley Act are thus translated into requirements for the Technology Infrastructure and thus directly impact IT's core responsibility areas.

It is fairly straightforward to assign the various available (and most likely already deployed) enterprise applications and technologies according to the various requirements of the Corporate Management Systems as described below:

Accelerated Reporting Requirement

- **Quickly Assembling Data:** This requirement is fulfilled mostly through Transaction Processing Systems, such as ERP, SCM and CRM. In these systems, each transaction the enterprise is involved in is captured at the point of the transaction itself. The systems are implemented such that the transaction cannot go through unless all the relevant data is incorporated into it[5].

  In many corporations, this kind of data might be captured through legacy or functionally-dedicated (single-module) transaction processing systems, such as sales order management systems, procurement systems, billing systems etc. In this case, the data is usually routed in some form to the "mother-ship" ERP system. But if the integration is not done properly, there is the possibility of a weakness at this point.

---

[4] Of course, it is possible to continue implementing several of the Corporate Management Systems without much technology. However, this will make them highly inefficient, ineffective, slow and prone to errors and deficiencies.

[5] This provides a form of control on the transaction as well as the data at the point of generation itself.

If the enterprise has several such disparate legacy or functionally-dedicated systems in place[6] then it is important to closely audit their integration with the core Financial and Accounting or ERP system.

- **Centralized Data Repository[7]:** This kind of data repository is inherently available in corporations that have an integrated ERP system in place. For other organizations, with heterogeneous technologies and business applications, the repository would exist if Data Warehouse Systems (and especially ETL tools, i.e. Extraction, Transformation and Loading tools) have been deployed and the appropriate meta-data architecture (i.e. centralized for small and medium enterprises, decentralized for large enterprises or distributed for enterprises that have gone through several mergers and acquisitions) suited to the organizational architecture were implemented.

  For very large organizations with multiple transaction systems and "data overlap"[8] problems, this can be supplemented with Enterprise Repositories.

- **Reporting and Analytical Systems:** The reporting systems deployed in the corporation are likely to be much more sophisticated than a typical MIS (Management Information System). However, an MIS would fulfill a lot of the reporting requirements. This does require the analysts to take the MIS reports, feed them into spreadsheets and then do their own analyses. Although this is prone to error and is person-dependent, it is a reasonably good solution for small and medium enterprises.

  An alternative approach would be to implement a lot of the analyses into pre-programmed Business Intelligence (BI) tools (such as OLAP, Data Mining,

---

[6] This is quite possible for a large organization with a long history that has gone through numerous mergers and acquisitions.

[7] Or: Centrally Accessible Data Repository.

[8] For example, the same customer information is available in slightly different formats in the ERP, CRM and SCM systems, but there is no simple automated way to decide that it is so.

and related Decision Support Tools) and let the analysts work out various analyses.

A new category of enterprise applications can be highly useful for providing reporting of "material events" in "real-time", namely the Business Activity Monitoring systems. Various enterprise applications have a module falling under this category and several dedicated applications in this category also exist.

Related classes of applications that will put "the real-time" information at the tips of the CEO and the CFO are the Executive Dashboards and the Business Performance Monitoring Systems and Operational Intelligence systems.

- **Report Distribution System or Document Management and Workflow Systems:** Although reporting requirements would be satisfied with a Report Distribution System, it is best to go for an Integrated (and versatile) Document Management and Workflow System. A DMS combined with a workflow system would enable the same solutions to be utilized for multiple requirements of Sarbanes-Oxley. Hence, this would be an ideal choice or even a "must-have"[9] for Sarbanes-Oxley compliance.

- **Public Information Distribution System:** This requirement can be taken care of by deploying Enterprise Information Portal Systems. These portals can disburse information to the appropriate stakeholders and investors, as well as to regulatory authorities. The portals do the job of "publishing" the appropriate documents and real-time alerts through proper access control systems after going through the pre-defined approval hierarchy, and post them automatically on to the enterprise websites on the Internet and the Intranet. Most Portal Systems also allow automatic notification emails and SMS alerts to be sent to the subscribed users.

A simplified alternative could be to have a basic website where important information is published, and

---

[9] Together with ERP and Enterprise Application Integration (EAI)

email notifications to various agencies and regulatory authorities are sent, in addition to electronic and hardcopy filings. Further, notifying investors and stakeholders via email newsletters can also fulfill several important requirements of Sarbanes-Oxley.

Certification Requirement

- **Data Capture System:** The automated solutions for these are essentially implemented using Transaction Processing Systems, either integrated applications such as ERP, CRM and SCM or functionally-dedicated ones, such as Sales Order Management System, Billing Systems, Lead Management Systems etc.
- **Document Capture System:** There are several Document Imaging and Capture solutions available with OCR (Optical Character Recognition), ICR (Intelligent Character Recognition) and IMR (Intelligent Mark Recognition) capabilities. Further, solutions exist for Form Identification and Recognition as well as for Structured and Unstructured Document Information Capture Solutions.
- **Secure Data and Document transfer:** There are several solutions for secure data and document transfer, such as various kinds of Encryption Technology and Digital Rights Management.

Internal Controls

- **Integration of Enterprise Applications:** Having an integrated ERP is the conceptually cleanest way of satisfying the requirement of seamless integration. Depending on where they are in terms of technology, this may or may not be a feasible option at the present.

  Fortunately, there are several other means to satisfy this requirement. Sharing data and documents in a centralized repository is one way to partially achieve this. There are a number of technologies available today for Enterprise Integration, namely Enterprise Application Integration, Web Services and Web Integration, Data Integration, Middleware, XML (or its several versions such as ebXML and XBRL) and Business Process Integration.

- **Security Systems**: Systems such as the Role Based Access Control System, Security Audit System, Encryption System, Policy Management software and Vulnerability Management software provide the basic security infrastructure required for Sarbanes-Oxley compliance.

Communications

The communications system required for the whistleblower protection and communication should be based on email, telephone and secure document management, and must ensure the anonymity, accessibility and objectivity of the communication and complaint tracking system put in place for whistleblower communications between the employees and the Audit Committee.

Business Processes Impacted by Sarbanes-Oxley

The Key Business Processes of the Enterprise are:

1. Marketing and Sales
   a. Invoicing
   b. Collections
   c. Sales Forecasting
2. Research, Design and Development
3. Purchasing and Subcontracting (Supply Chain)
   a. Ordering
   b. Payments
   c. Material Logistics
4. Production Planning and Control
   a. Raw Material and WIP Inventory Management
   b. Quality System
   c. Labor Management
5. Distribution and Warehousing
   a. Finished Goods Inventory Management
   b. Warehouse Management
   c. Dealer Logistics

6. After Sales Service

These Business Processes form the core processes of the live enterprise. With the exception of business processes 2 and 6, that is, "Research, Design and Development" and "After Sales Service", all the other Business Processes are directly impacted by Sarbanes-Oxley. The systems that are used to manage these, whether manual or automated, will be impacted. Further, comprehensive, confident and convenient compliance with sections 302 and 404 would dictate that these systems be seamlessly integrated with each other; ideally, they would be incorporated into one single system, for example, an integrated ERP.

However, many large public companies are the result of several mergers or acquisitions, spread out globally in several countries and involved in diverse product lines. This typically results in a jig-saw of IT systems that are incompatible legacy systems of the merging companies. Further, each country location can typically be expected to have a different instance of IT systems and each product line function would be treated as a different business unit and would have their own IT system. This complexity poses its own set of challenges.

TECHNOLOGIES IMPACTED BY SARBANES-OXLEY

Even in a simplified IT environment, it is expected that the CRM system, managing the sales and distribution, the SCM system, typically managing the procurement supply chain and sometimes managing the distribution or demand chain, the ERP system, managing the financials and accounting, Internal Controls, inventory and production, would all be different IT systems. Add to these the numerous supporting IT systems for the several subsidiary business processes and the picture of the various data islands in the enterprise begins to emerge. It is to be expected that the data from these disparate systems will not reflect the same view of reality. What data represents the true picture of reality is anybody's guess.

However, the CEO and the CFO have to sign on personal liability and risk that the financial reports are accurate and reflect the true picture to the best of their knowledge and that they have checked the internal controls supporting the financial processes. This puts the pressure on the CIO in turn to make sure that the key business processes are properly implemented and that the data is accurate and secure. How to accomplish this will be discussed in detail later.

SEPARATE VENDOR HYPE FROM REALITY

Vendors are hoping to cash-in on the FUD[10]-factor created by Sarbanes-Oxley and, for obvious reasons, there is some level of:

- **Fear:** Sarbanes-Oxley provides for personal liability and imprisonment of the CEO and CFO in case of deviation from the Sarbanes-Oxley-prescribed rules and regulations.
- **Uncertainty:** The exact steps to be taken to comply with Sarbanes-Oxley are still uncertain. According to AMR Research, about 80% of CIOs are not clear about the exact significance of Sarbanes-Oxley for their company.
- **Doubt:** There are concerns about the precise impact of Sarbanes-Oxley on the enterprise, the CEO, the CFO and the CIO and the extent to which Sarbanes-Oxley will be enforced and the sections that the SEC will enforce.

The way to separate vendor hype from reality is to do your own analysis. There is no simple way to separate hype from reality. In general, in the case of all established vendors, there is a fine line between hype and reality. Vendors are an important source of relevant information and a lot of that information cannot be dismissed as hype.

---

[10] Fear, Uncertainty and Doubt

However, especially when the issue is of compliance with laws such as Sarbanes-Oxley, it is important for the CIO, CEO and CFO to have an extremely skeptical mind to prevent the implications of noncompliance from clouding their thinking.

The way to cut through the vendor hype, or any other hype, is to ask specific questions and get into the details of the service and product offerings. The devil of hype hides within the details. The following questions are provided as a guideline to ask the vendor about their products and/or services:

Vendor/Product Due-Diligence Checklist

Which section(s) of Sarbanes-Oxley does the product/ service relate to?
How does it support compliance with that/those section(s) of Sarbanes-Oxley?
Are there other classes of products from other vendors that also claim to provide compliance?
Will the vendor provide a written statement that the product provides compliance with Sarbanes-Oxley?
How does it improve upon the existing system? What deficiency in the existing system does it address?
Is there a simpler and more inexpensive way to rectify this deficiency?
Has the vendor worked with "Sarbanes-Oxley experts" to develop the system?
What other changes will need to be made if the product is purchased and implemented? Will it impact several other systems which are already in place? Will all of these need to be changed?
Have any "Sarbanes-Oxley experts" certified or endorsed the said product as "Sarbanes-Oxley compliant"?

SARBANES-OXLEY COMPLIANCE AS AN IT PROJECT

It is imperative that Sarbanes-Oxley compliance be viewed by the CIO as an IT Project. A project can be

124

defined as a list of activities to achieve a desired outcome or goal using predefined, fixed resources and completed within a given time frame. This will help in the implementation of Sarbanes-Oxley, using IT within the desired timeline, with well-understood goals and within budget. The risk of project failure is reduced. Sarbanes-Oxley compliance is one project where failure is not an option.

PERSPECTIVE ON SARBANES-OXLEY GOALS

How the CIO chooses the goal of the Sarbanes-Oxley compliance project for IT is an important question. There are several goals the CIO may choose from:

- **The Obvious:** The goal for Sarbanes-Oxley compliance using IT as set by the CEO or the CFO.
- **The Easy:** Vendor-recommended Sarbanes-Oxley compliant product implementation.
- **The Mandatory:** Foolproof implementation of Sarbanes-Oxley Compliant Key Enterprise Technologies (SOCKET™) across the organization and any change in the SOCKET Ecosystem should be arrived at via a structured approach, without affecting the Sarbanes-Oxley compliance of the system.
- **The Proactive:** Achieve strategic enterprise goals through proper encapsulation of Key Business Processes (KBPs) in a Sarbanes-Oxley-Compliant Key Enterprise Technology (SOCKET) Ecosystem.

CIOs will have to choose the goal that is appropriate for their current situation and constraints. However, given sufficient resources and operational freedom, it is best to choose the proactive goal. The easy goal might be the one to go for where the vendor's claims have been verified by the Corporate Sarbanes-Oxley Compliance Team and have been found to satisfy Sarbanes-Oxley compliance, and the vendor has successfully implemented their product in a company in a similar industry sector. The obvious goal will have to be adhered to in any case. The mandatory goal is the best way to ensure that all important processes for Sarbanes-Oxley compliance using technology have been followed.

STEPS FOR SARBANES-OXLEY COMPLIANCE

The process towards compliance begins with a broad-level conversation with the compliance team led by the Chief Compliance Officer (CCO)[11] or equivalent. The detailed process for Sarbanes-Oxley compliance for IT is provided later. Here, we give a brief overview of the main steps involved. The compliance team should include the CEO, the CFO, the CIO and the CCO, and other relevant personnel. This team should prepare the *Vision for Compliance*, the *Timeline for Compliance* (the internal time frame for compliance with various sections), and the *Resources for Compliance* (the resources and costs the company is able and willing to commit to the compliance effort) documents. They must then follow the *Strategy for Compliance*.

This compliance strategy will prescribe the mix of people, processes and technology that will be required to achieve compliance. The processes will need to be audited and analyzed. The extent of automation, the number of IT systems and the number of people required to implement each of these processes will need to be studied.

The processes themselves might need to be modified to provide for designing fundamentally more secure and controlled instances of them. The control

---

[11] The CCO will usually be a senior professional with a legal background and who has an understanding of enterprise operations at the broad or big-picture level and also at the ground level. S/he should have the appropriate authority within the company, and the CEO, the CFO and the CIO should be accessible to him/her. The key personnel in the enterprise should also believe in his/her capability and expertise. This person can be either a consultant or a "home-grown" officer with a long history in the organization.

126

features in each of the IT systems will need to be configured to attain the desired controls. The remaining control deficiencies can either be addressed through implementing new IT systems, or can be done manually by creating new control procedures, documenting them and assigning responsibilities to the appropriate personnel. The basic principle behind the proper design of these controls requires that a sufficiently large number of people be involved in the controls to prevent the possibility of a collusion of people being able to circumvent the control. However, this requirement has to be balanced by the requirement of making the process efficient.

There is another possibility for fundamentally changing the architecture of the IT system and acquiring completely new software (possibly a single instance ERP) into which all the processes and the data are migrated. The chances are high that this kind of system will be Sarbanes-Oxley compliant. However, the chances of a single instance ERP being able to take care of all the diverse needs of the global, multi-product, sufficiently diversified enterprise are very low[12]. Even if such an ERP exists, migrating to it will be an extremely high-risk, time-consuming and costly venture; exactly the kind of thing Sarbanes-Oxley, in spirit, was designed to save the investors from!

Ten Steps to Sarbanes-Oxley Compliance

The following provides a step-by-step process for achieving Sarbanes-Oxley compliance in the Enterprise:

(To download a copy of this worksheet, visit www.SarbanesOxleyGuide.com)

Seq.	Process Step	Time-frame	Budget
1.	Understand key sections of Sarbanes-Oxley, especially Sec. 302 and 404.		
2.	Decide to create a		

---

[12] This might however be a longer-term goal for medium-sized companies to achieve compliance in the medium to long-term

	Sarbanes-Oxley Compliant Key Enterprise Technology (SOCKET™) Ecosystem.		
3.	Develop a Project Plan for the SOCKET Ecosystem.		
4.	Get the approval of the CEO and the CFO for creating the SOCKET Ecosystem.		
5.	Identify and select the top level of the Sarbanes-Oxley (SOCKET) compliance committee.		
6.	Conduct a Sarbanes-Oxley requirements analysis.		
7.	Implement "Sarbanes-Oxley Compliance for IT" or SOCKET process at the pilot site.		
8.	Replicate this success story at all the locations.		
9.	Audit and confirm that Sarbanes-Oxley compliance has been achieved.		
10.	Put an ongoing SOCKET audit and implementation process and team in place to ensure continued Sarbanes-Oxley compliance.		

In general, an initial business process analysis (BPA) identifies areas of:

- Inefficiency in information flow
- Inaccuracy and security vulnerabilities in the transaction, analysis and reporting systems
- Ineffective internal controls

- Deficiencies in real-time reporting and control monitoring capability for CEOs and CFOs
- Inappropriate data, document and record storage for the long-term (at least 7 years), and includes disaster recovery infrastructure requirements
- Communication systems inefficiency or security vulnerability

The BPA (business process analysis) exercise needs to be followed by a BPR (business process reengineering) to reengineer the identified deficiencies and then a BPM (business process management) system to help implement the new business processes and monitor them.

Total Cost of Compliance (TCC)

The total cost of compliance should be calculated in a manner similar to calculating the "Total Cost" of any project or product. For this, we need to look at the complete process for compliance. Of course, we will restrict discussion here to the costs of the IT department.

The IT department will need to form a SOCKET team. This SOCKET team will have to spend time, effort, and resources on the compliance project. Further, the SOCKET team may need to acquire IT products and/or services that will require additional investment. Total cost is calculated taking into account the required people, processes and technologies. Cash flow, IRR and other related calculations are done for financial justifications.

This is one of the most crucial steps in a SOCKET implementation. All the inputs related to people, processes and technology must be fully understood. Each Gap, Risk Control Area and Internal Control Systems area is analyzed in detail and for each identified initiative, a detailed project plan is made. For each project, the requirement of resources, time frame, deliverables, budget and control measures are worked out. For more details refer to the **SOCKET TCC Calculator** spreadsheet at www.SarbanesOxleyGuide.com. It is one of the most valuable tools you will use as you embark on your Sarbanes-Oxley compliance journey.

SARBANES-OXLEY AND THE SEC

A number of recent media articles suggest that the SEC has watered down the requirements and that there is not much to be done to comply with the SEC rulings on Sarbanes-Oxley. Is this the best approach or is the best approach yet to be seen? The SEC might have watered down the Sarbanes-Oxley Act in implementation, but which organization would you like to risk being the first to test these waters?

To play it safe, the best recourse is to take the strong interpretation of Sarbanes-Oxley and to comply with that. This is recommended, since what Sarbanes-Oxley mandates is good business practice in any case. However, given financial or other resource constraints it might be a reasonable decision to adhere to the bare minimum required according to SEC recommendations. When choosing the latter strategy, it is important to understand the risks involved and decide on a strong interpretation of Sarbanes-Oxley compliance in the long term.

CHAPTER 13
THE ENTERPRISE TECHNOLOGY ECOSYSTEM

THE ENTERPRISE TECHNOLOGY ECOSYSTEM PERSPECTIVE

The SOCKET Framework can be viewed as an "ecosystem" framework. This means that all the components of the ecosystem are treated as important and critical. A change in any one of the components will result in a change in the way the ecosystem works. At a particular point in time, the ecosystem might be optimized or tuned for accomplishing a certain set of business or technology objectives, or for delivering a particular set of functionalities exceptionally well. As the business environment changes, the ecosystem needs to be optimized for changes.

The ecosystem framework provides for an organic and evolving view of the enterprise architecture. The conventional enterprise architecture view is static and mechanistic. In the conventional view, the business objectives are assumed as a given and the technology architecture is developed to optimize for achieving the business objectives.

In the ecosystem framework, it is recognized that the business ecosystem[13] itself is dynamic and hence, the business objectives are ever-changing. Further, the technology components themselves are continuously evolving. Hence, the enterprise architecture should be designed to be evolving and adaptive; thus, it has to be viewed as an ecosystem.

---

[13] See Death of Competition, James Moore and Zeleny *et al*, 'Moving from the Age of Specialization to the Era of Integration', *Human Systems Management*, vol. 9, (1990) pp. 153-171.

The Business-Technology Optimization Dilemma

In a static, inorganic view of the Enterprise Technology Infrastructure, it means completely redesigning the new architecture from scratch, hoping to keep as much of the existing technology unchanged as possible. This static viewpoint yields an infrastructure that is then optimized for the new conditions. By the time the changes are in place, the conditions have changed again. Hence, the technology infrastructure always lags behind the business objectives.

The solution to this dilemma is to view the enterprise as a dynamic, organic ecosystem. The ecosystem perspective emphasizes the idea that the technology infrastructure is dynamic, and although stable or tuned or optimized at any given point in time, it will eventually change again. The key is to change it in a controlled manner, at a rate of change suitable to the enterprise, and in the direction that the enterprise business objectives dictate.

This requires viewing the technology ecosystem as a whole. The technology ecosystem has to be viewed as an infrastructure layer supporting the business processes of the enterprise in the business ecosystem, both within and outside the enterprise. The purpose of the technology ecosystem is to make the business processes faster, more efficient and more effective.

When the business requirements change, such as in the case of new regulations like Sarbanes-Oxley, the technology ecosystem needs to be reviewed in the context of the new business ecosystem. The new business process ecosystem needs to be analyzed. The SOCKET ecosystem, for example, dictates several rules:

1. **Section 103:** Preservation of documents and records for seven years to mirror the storage by the auditors.
2. **Section 302:** All the financial data should be accurate.
3. **Section 404:** The internal controls must be in place and auditable.
4. **Section 409:** Requires real-time reporting of "material" events that impact current and projected

financials. This makes it important to apply these newly important business requirements to the ecosystem and change them to suit it accordingly.

Should that be taken to imply that a completely new technology infrastructure is required? The short answer is "no". One of the fundamental premises of this guidebook is: *80% of the companies already have at least 80% of the technology required to achieve SOX compliance.*

However, adapting this ecosystem to the new business and regulatory stimuli (or requirements) will need a detailed audit of the infrastructure. The output or work product of that audit will be a report giving the gap analysis of what the ideal system for the current business requirement of Sarbanes-Oxley compliance requires and how well the current system provides for compliance.

The next step will be to compile a reengineering report. This report will outline how many of the requirements from the gap analysis can be satisfied by reorganizing the existing technology infrastructure and which of them may require new technology. With this report in hand, the reorganized technology infrastructure is created and then the remaining gaps are filled using new technologies. Even here, a lot can be accomplished by procuring or developing simple patches/fixes and only a few requirements will require completely new technology.

The Enterprise Technology Ecosystem Framework is designed to adaptively and continuously align the enterprise business and technology goals and operations in a continuously changing business ecosystem. The framework allows the CIO to visualize the enterprise IT infrastructure from a holistic perspective and to see its interaction or relationship to changes in the business ecosystem; e.g. Sarbanes-Oxley and the financial business processes that it affects.

CHAPTER 14
IMPLEMENTING THE SOCKET
FRAMEWORK

Sarbanes-Oxley has changed the existing Business Ecosystem by impacting some of the key business processes that have, in turn, had an impact on the accuracy of financial reports and internal controls on financials. These business processes create or capture relevant financial information through software applications running on specific technology platforms. The SOCKET framework enables us to visualize how all these aspects work together.

The SOCKET framework assists and enables the CIO to visualize the enterprise IT infrastructure holistically and to gain insight into its interaction and relationship to Sarbanes-Oxley and the key financially relevant business processes.

THE "SPECIES" OR COMPONENTS OF THE ENTERPRISE TECHNOLOGY ECOSYSTEM

The business ecosystem, including the regulatory environment, defines the fundamental requirements of the enterprise technology ecosystem. The enterprise technology ecosystem is an inter-dependent system of various technology components, including hardware, software, networks, standards, and protocols, amongst others.

The enterprise technology ecosystem has to be designed in such a way so as to allow frequent and continuous changes in the business ecosystem. The newly important business processes should easily be automated and made available through the existing technology ecosystem or should require buying limited new technology components to manifest the particular set of business processes. In the most challenging case, it should require buying an IT system that seamlessly blends in with the rest of the existing technology ecosystem without causing serious repercussions through the rest of the enterprise.

This, in essence, is the goal that the enterprise technology ecosystem framework strives towards.

The species of the enterprise technology ecosystem are the hardware, the software, the network, the standards, and the protocols. The business processes that utilize these keep changing with time. Hence, these components should be flexible and adaptable enough to manifest any new business processes that will become important in the future.

Interaction of the Species

The components interact with each other through interfaces. These interfaces should be such that they can be made to easily interact with any of the other species or components without restriction or significant effort. This calls for following "open" standards in general, or de facto industry standards. Further, if vendor lock-in is to be avoided to avert potentially disastrous vendor-dependency, then appropriate standards that are supported by multiple vendors must be chosen.

Organic and Evolving Nature

Every CIO is clear that the enterprise technology ecosystem components or species are continuously evolving and changing. The vendors providing these components try to make these better and faster and try to provide more features with each new generation of the species. In itself, this is good progress. However, taking the enterprise ecosystem as a whole, the introduction of new species causes instability in the ecosystem. Each new species requires changes in several business processes and the other species it interacts with, in terms of requiring new training for the personnel involved in its implementation, use and maintenance.

If it is a new piece of software, it might require newer hardware, more disk space, and better and faster networks. Sometimes, it could require that different standards or protocols be adapted. Data might have to be migrated from older formats or systems to new formats and systems. The implementation teams will have to be trained on the configuration capabilities; the users will have to be trained on the features and functionality; and the

136

maintenance team will have to be trained on the new administration and maintenance requirements and functionality of the new species.

All of this results in decreased productivity during migration time, extra effort from IT personnel for deployment and system migration, and other business personnel to adapt to the new way of conducting the business process.

Benefits of the Ecosystem Perspective

The ecosystem perspective keeps these issues firmly in the limelight, emphasizing foresight, synthesis and analysis before taking any technology-buying initiative. It brings a very high level of perspective to the planning and buying decisions, keeping the technology decisions closely aligned to the business drivers. If the business ecosystem dictates, the first attempt will be to reconfigure the existing technology ecosystem to achieve the desired effects. If, however, this does not seem possible within the constraints, then a buying decision can be made.

What is to be bought and how will it fit into the current technology ecosystem? How will it tie-down or free up the enterprise to change its business models or processes in response to the changing business ecosystem? What will be the repercussions of the new species on the existing ecosystem?

This ecosystem framework forces reflection on such questions and issues before the introduction of a new technology species in the existing enterprise technology ecosystem.

COSO FRAMEWORK

The SOCKET framework has to be supplemented by the COSO (Committee of Sponsoring Organizations of the Treadway Commission) framework for achieving Sarbanes-Oxley compliance. The COSO framework for Internal Controls has been suggested by the SEC as a possible framework for evaluating the Internal Controls. This framework is relevant to Section 404 of the Sarbanes-Oxley Act.

There are three main objectives for determining which Internal Controls are to be applied:

- Efficiency and effectiveness of operations
- Financial reporting reliability
- Regulatory compliance

For each of these objectives, the five components of Internal Controls are:

- Control Environment: Corporate control culture and consciousness
- Risk Assessment: Assessment of risk factors for each objective
- Control Activities: Corporate policies, procedures and processes that ensure the span of Management control throughout the enterprise
- Information and Communication: Implementation of key business processes for efficient capture, storage and distribution of relevant information required for efficient operations
- Monitoring: Ongoing or periodic internal control assessment processes

The above components of internal controls are evaluated for each objective at the unit level (functional) and the activity level (business process).

This framework is discussed to give you a feel for the overall internal audit that the Corporate Sarbanes-Oxley Audit Team will have to carry out in its evaluation of internal controls. Since one of the core components of internal controls, according to COSO, is information and communication, this will be directly related to the IT infrastructure of the enterprise. Further, the functional and business process level assessments will also result in the assessment of the technology infrastructure in supporting those requirements. Hence, it is important that selected personnel (i.e. both the SOCKET Audit Team and the SOCKET Implementation Team) become conversant with

COSO and how it applies to Sarbanes-Oxley and the technology infrastructure of the enterprise.

IT controls such as security, physical access control over digital assets and corporate knowledge, business continuity and disaster recovery, control on the implementation of new applications and technology; modifications to existing applications and technology, retirement or maintenance of existing applications and technology, and authorization to personnel for accessing only relevant information technology assets are some of the enterprise-wide controls that are relevant.

SOCKET TECHNOLOGIES

For achieving a SOCKET Ecosystem, the following are some of the general principles to adhere to:

- Centralized (or centrally accessible) data repository
- Centralized (or centrally accessible) document repository
- Pervasive logical and physical security infrastructure
- Pervasive enterprise hierarchical access control to IT and information assets
- Access to information assets and IT to personnel, restricted to the required domain of their responsibilities
- Secure and accurate mechanisms for the transfer of data, document and other information assets from one layer or species of technology to another
- Enterprise-wide business continuity plans and disaster recovery procedures for the enterprise technology ecosystem

TRANSACTIONAL SYSTEMS: ERP, SCM, CRM

The key business processes of an enterprise, such as sales and procurement, can be automated using transactional systems. Earlier, and to some extent, even today, specialized software or systems were developed that were dedicated to automating a particular aspect of a key business process, such as, a sales order management system for processing sales orders. After the sales order was approved, it would be passed on for further processing to the dispatch department where the data would be re-keyed into another transactional system for warehouse management. Once the inventory levels in the warehouse would reach a pre-defined level, the warehouse management system would generate an alert and a pre-defined number of units would be requested from the production department. The production department would then be alerted and would work on replenishing the warehouse to the desired level. The production department would then check their own production planning system and order the required amount of raw material from the stores. Once the raw material inventory in the stores reached a certain level, the stores management system would generate an alert and a re-order of a predefined number of units of raw materials would be passed onto the respective suppliers.

In this way, there were latencies in information transfer at each stage and the business processes of the enterprise were implemented in a very inefficient manner. Further, there were errors during the re-keying of data. The designs of the "source" systems reports and the "target or sink" systems' input forms would inevitably be slightly different resulting in a loss or distortion of data. Any enterprise-wide holistic analysis would be inherently difficult due to the sheer effort required to consolidate all the relevant data from all the legacy systems into a single system. Hence, the enterprise was not "self-aware", only the sub-processes automated by single software were each "self-aware" and open to analysis and self-improvement.

To circumvent these problems, the concept of ERP (Enterprise Resource Planning) was born. ERP refers to an enterprise-wide transactional system capturing the key business process data at the point of generation. The core business processes of finance; production planning and inventory management were automated and encapsulated in a single system. The dream of ERP was, of course, to

140

embody all the key business processes and present a single transactional framework and database.

As it turns out, there were other key business processes such as sales process, customer interaction, supplier interaction etc. This gave rise to two other key categories of enterprise software: CRM (Customer Relationship Management) and SCM (Supply Chain Management).

Today, it is generally accepted that ERP is the core transactional system providing automation of the enterprise's internal business processes, SCM provides automation for the back-end or supply-side of the enterprise and CRM provides automation for the front-end or demand-side of the enterprise. Thus, this trio of systems forms the core transactional system that completes the value chain and key business processes of the "Extended Enterprise" forming a closed loop.

This closed loop of key business processes is what Sarbanes-Oxley impacts the most. Any glitch, anywhere along this value chain, will immediately propagate through the rest of the value chain. This could result in a loss of revenue due to loss of sales, since some aspect of the demand could not be fulfilled in time. In many cases, this may even threaten the very existence of the enterprise.

Before Sarbanes-Oxley

In 2000, Ericsson, the Swedish manufacturer of mobile phones, faced a sales shortfall of nearly $1billion. This was partly the result of a fire in a factory of one of its crucial microchip suppliers. Ericsson came to know about it more than a week later. Nokia came to know about it even before being formally informed by the supplier and had already taken action by contacting alternative suppliers![14]

---

[14] Creating Resilient Supply Chains: A Practical Guide, www.cranfield.ac.uk/som/scr

The above case study starkly demonstrates the crucial role automation of the key business processes will play in Sarbanes-Oxley compliance. All of these processes have significant impact on the financials of the company by affecting sales, revenues, supply, inventory and costs.

Even Alan Greenspan, in his testimony to the Congress in 2001, emphasized the benefits of SCM and related software:

"New technologies for supply-chain management and flexible manufacturing imply that businesses can perceive imbalances in inventories at a very early stage - virtually in real time - and can cut production promptly in response to the developing signs of unintended inventory building."[15]

The following is typically how the business cycle operates: CRM sales order creation triggers the value chain. The order goes through to the fulfillment management module and a product is dispatched to the customer. Once the product leaves the warehouse, this information goes into the Warehouse Management module of the ERP system and triggers a requirement for one more piece of the just-dispatched product. This triggers a requirement in the Production Planning module of the ERP system and in turn in the Stores module of the ERP for the raw materials related to the product. The dispatch of the raw materials to the production line creates a requirement in the Raw Material Inventory management module of the Supply Chain Management system and this is propagated throughout the tiers of the supplier's enterprise systems.

---

[15] http://www.federalreserve.gov/boarddocs/hh/2001/february/testimony.htm

The weak links in this information value chain are where the information leaves the CRM system and enters the ERP, and where it leaves the ERP and enters the SCM system. It is possible that data loss or distortion could take place at these points[16][17]?

There is also the risk of loss of internal controls, since there exist possibilities of supplies being ordered through the SCM system at costs for which there might be no customers in the marketplace; or orders being booked from customers which cannot be fulfilled within the time period promised; or products being planned for which raw material cannot be obtained within the time period planned. These are inherent risks of having different systems for these processes. The following case study provides an example of these kinds of risks[18]:

> *In the mid-1990s, the Swedish car manufacturer, Volvo, found itself with excessive stocks of green cars. To move them along, the sales and marketing departments began offering attractive special deals, so green cars started to sell. But nobody had told the manufacturing department about the promotions. It noted the increase in sales, read it as a sign that consumers had started to like green, and ramped up production.*

These risks could result in violation of Sec. 404. Further, due to different information on, for example, the current finished goods, work-in-progress, and raw materials

---

[16] J. Woods, A. White, K. Peterson, and M. Jimenez, Gartner Research Note. Demand Chain Management Synchronizes CRM and SCM, October 28, 2002.

[17] Count the Money when Sales and Marketing Work with Logistics Simon Pollard, UK Senior Analyst, AMR Research, October 2001

[18] http://www.economist.com/surveys/displayStory.cfm?Story_id=949105 and; Ultimate Enterprise Value Creation Using Demand-Based Management: Hau Lee, Stanford Global Supply Chain Management Forum September, 2001.

in the different systems it could result in financial inaccuracies resulting in violation of Sec. 302. Also, if the "glitches" anywhere along the value chain of the three systems are not brought to the immediate attention of the CEO and the CFO, this could result in loss of revenues, and this situation could end up with a violation of Sec. 409 since "material" events occurring in the company would not be immediately informed to the investors and regulatory agencies by the CEO and CFO.

But the fact remains that these three transactional systems have reduced the points of failure by orders of magnitude and Sarbanes-Oxley compliance will be much easier with these systems in place (or at least some of these in place, especially ERP) than without it.

CFP Research Services and Cap Gemini Ernst and Young surveyed 265 financial executives in 2002. The survey showed that 98% of the respondents had ERP systems that were not fully integrated with other applications and 71% felt that this could not be achieved even within the next 3 years.[19]

It is obvious that there is no way to obtain completely accurate financial reports without a full integration between all ERP and financially relevant software applications. How companies will be able to address Sarbanes-Oxley section 302 for accurate financial reporting without such integration is anybody's guess. Further, it seems quite difficult to comply with Section 404 in terms of proper internal controls when the financial systems themselves are not properly integrated. In fact, it is virtually assured that the internal controls will have weaknesses. The best course the CEOs and CFOs have then is to conduct a proper assessment of the weaknesses and file such a report with a projected timeline for eliminating these weaknesses.

---

[19] CFOs: Driving Finance transformation for the 21st century, Cap Gemini Ernst & Young http://www.ca.cgey.com/ knowledge_centre/insights/findrivingfinancetransformation.pdf

Any quick-fix attempts will only result in weak internal controls. However, there are solutions to these problems:

Configure the controls already present in the existing software systems. Consolidate and reconcile, as far as possible, the data in the multiple ERP systems or other existing transaction systems. Use financial reporting and business intelligence systems that use data from centralized data repositories and that consolidate the data from the ERP, SCM, CRM and other systems. Further, these should be supported by Executive Dashboards and Business Activity Monitoring systems that are programmed to provide alerts on the occurrence of "material" events.

ANALYTICAL AND REPORTING SYSTEMS

Even today, a majority of companies, including Fortune 500 companies, use spreadsheets to perform various analyses on their corporate data and create reports for management. The likelihood of introducing errors in any reasonably large-sized spreadsheet model is more than 90%[20] [21].

Section 302

According to The Hackett Group's survey in 2003, 91% of companies are not confident in their reporting and forecasting data. 47% still rely on spreadsheets for their reporting. This means collating data from a large number of sources into the spreadsheets. This in itself significantly increases the odds that there will be corrupt/incorrect data in the spreadsheets. Combine this with data on spreadsheet errors and the resulting reports are virtually guaranteed to

---

[20] Freeman, D. (1996). "How to Make Spreadsheets Error-Proof." Journal of Accountancy, 181(5), 75-77.

[21] KPMG Management Consulting, "Supporting the Decision Maker - A Guide to the Value of Business Modeling," press release, July 30, 1998.
http://www.kpmg.co.uk/uk/services/manage/press/970605a.html.

be inaccurate. So, in fact, the CEO or CFO can confidently certify that the financial reports are <u>not</u> correct!

Further, Hackett Group data also reveals that 89% of the CFOs feel that the spreadsheet-based systems cannot comply with the internal control and audit requirements. Hence, this exposes the CFOs and CEOs under section 404 in addition to section 302.

Under such circumstances, the CEO and the CFO cannot confidently certify the Sec. 302 and Sec. 404 mandated financial and internal control reports. The enterprise has to move toward a financial reporting model that does not involve data moving from application to application through manual re-keying or copy-and-pastes where errors can be introduced.

An ideal solution is to have good reporting that integrates data from all the major transactional systems or from the central data repository and provides data in a manner that allows consistency checks across the data from the various systems and audit traces of the source of the data.

The data entering this repository has to be checked for accuracy and the repository must have access control and security. All the financial reports would then be generated out of this central repository.

Another strategy is to obtain a reporting tool that has good features for transformation and visualization and to use it in conjunction with a centralized data repository. Most OLAP (On-Line Analytical Processing) tools have excellent reporting features and it is often suggested that this may be the best approach to achieve compliance with Sec. 302 and Sec. 404 as well as to obtain business insights into the way the business is performing, thereby creating an infrastructure for sustained competitive advantage.

Real-time Executive Reporting: Section 409

Disclosure of material changes to business within two business days. The fundamental requirement for this is that the company and its management should become aware of material changes in real-time. For most enterprises, this in itself seems difficult to attain, let alone filing appropriate disclosures and making them public.

146

Hence, the relevant information should reach top management in real-time and the proper analysis of the information or data needs to be carried out in real-time as well. The analysis of sales and payment data in real-time, for example, can help with triggering appropriate alerts in real-time and thereby enable management to file disclosures within the stipulated two business days.

There is an opinion that the nature of a majority of the "material" events listed by the SEC is such that they would not be part of the IT systems and that the CEO and CFO would come to know about them through some other means. Consider the following "material" events listed by the SEC:

#1: Change in control
#6: Publication of financial statements and exhibits
#8: Any disclosure under Regulation FD
#11: Results of operations and financial condition
#12: "Other materially important events"
#5 (new): Termination or reduction of a business relationship with a customer that constitutes a specified amount of the company's revenues
#9 (new): Events triggering a direct or contingent financial obligation that is material to the company, including any default or acceleration of an obligation.

All of these can be interpreted broadly around several events that could come to notice through IT systems in place in the enterprise. #1 could occur if access is granted to someone not authorized either intentionally or unintentionally, #6 could occur through automated publications using enterprise portals, and #11 and #12 could mean almost any operational event if it has a large financial impact. For example, this could be interpreted to be anything that could materially affect the business of the company, including events like a fire at Ericsson's supplier factory resulting in major supply problems.

Since 11 new material events have been added to the 9 material events already specified, the reporting systems should be configured and tuned to track potential cases and alert the management before such material events occur. This will help the management be ready with the disclosure reports almost immediately. The best course of action of course, when the event may not be favorable to the company's business, is to put management's focus on preventing such an event from taking place.

For example, if it appears that a major customer is reducing or is on the path to reducing their buying from the company, top management can be alerted and they can focus on preventing this situation, or in case it cannot be prevented, be ready to find alternate customers and take appropriate actions including filing disclosures when the triggering event does occur. Similarly, in the event that payment from a customer appears to be getting delayed, a real-time reporting system would track the delay before it reaches the position of a "write-off." Or a major supplier being unable to supply a crucial component or part on time. This would, again, send a real-time alert and prevent a material event, which could substantially reduce sales revenues.

Section 403

Reporting insider trading within two business days and posting it on the company website within one business day. What is required here is a reporting system such as a Business Activity Monitoring System or Business Performance Monitoring System or an Executive Dashboard. These systems can be configured to alert the key executives to potential threats and assist them in understanding whether these are "material" events or not.

DATA WAREHOUSING

Throughout this guidebook, through various reasoning approaches, one of the key points that keeps emerging is that a centralized data repository is a "must-have" tool for running a better business as well as for achieving Sarbanes-Oxley compliance. A data warehouse provides such a centralized data repository that can consolidate the data islands spread across the Enterprise Ecosystem in various transactional and other functional automation systems.

148

According to a 2001 survey by PWC:

> "Three-quarters [of the 600 companies across US, Australia and UK surveyed] reported significant problems as a result of defective data, with a third failing to bill or collect receivables as a result[22]."

The problem of "data cleansing" will have to be addressed even after using the ETL tools for Extraction, Transformation and Loading of the data. This is not a trivial problem and should be focused on very carefully before implementing a data warehouse. However, once this difficult exercise is completed and the Enterprise is confident about its data quality, the Sarbanes-Oxley certifications of financial accuracy can be signed. Further, it will provide a competitive advantage to the company against its competitors to work with high quality data.

One area of data quality control is at the time of data entry, specifically IT users who enter the data at the point of information or data creation. In most cases, this happens via input screens in ERP and other transactional systems. It is critical that these users be well trained and made aware of the importance of keying in accurate data and that a monitoring and control system be put in place to enforce good data entry quality. This then helps eliminate one major hindrance in certifying internal controls in accordance with Sec. 404. This will require data warehouse systems that provide bi-directional interaction, i.e. putting data into the warehouse, as well as accessing the data into the transactional systems from the data warehouse. This also ensures the re-use of pre-existing information, e.g. customers who are already present in the CRM system, and thereby eliminates the risk of incorrect data entry in the ERP system, e.g. re-entry of that customer information.

OLAP

In a Sarbanes-Oxley compliant environment, this data warehouse would be connected to an OLAP engine and other business intelligence systems. The various

---

[22] Global Data Management Survey 2001, PwC.

financial and analysis reports would be generated from this OLAP engine. Depending on various criteria, "trigger" alerts would be generated and sent to the appropriate senior managers.

OLAP provides management with drill-down capabilities down to the transaction-level data, which contributes to various aggregated information that is provided in disclosure reports to the regulatory authorities. This can provide tremendous confidence to the CEOs and CFOs on the quality and accuracy of the financial reports.

There exist Business Intelligence and Business Performance Management systems that make it possible for the Board or the C-level executives to get views on the Key Performance Indicators, and further, to drill down to the lower levels to see where the data is coming from and then deconstruct it. This drill-down capability goes down to the actual transaction level reports.

Data Mining

This is a tool/technique that does not have direct applicability to the section of the Sarbanes-Oxley Act, but it helps improve the performance of the business in an enterprise that has a large amount of good-quality data in a centralized data warehouse, and thereby contributes to the intent of the Act.

Data Mining can reveal new patterns and correlations between sets of data that might not seem to have any direct relationship to each other. This can potentially provide new hypotheses on the cause-and-effect relations throughout the Enterprise Value Chain. This will help in improving internal controls for:

- **Sec. 404:** Data Mining can be a useful tool for internal auditing of the internal controls in the hands of a good forensic accountant. It can reveal whether someone has tampered with the data using the frequencies of real data.
- **Sec 409:** Data Mining can also potentially alert the Enterprise by detecting unforeseen patterns, if any "material" events might have already taken place or might be in the offing.

150

KNOWLEDGE MANAGEMENT: DOCUMENT AND RECORDS MANAGEMENT

According to some estimates, more than 70% of the documents owned by an enterprise are in digital format and might never be seen in hardcopy. Document Management or Enterprise Information Management is perhaps one of the most important of the enterprise solutions that will provide a solution to the various requirements of Sarbanes-Oxley. Several sections of Sarbanes-Oxley have a direct bearing on the manner in which the digital documents/records of the enterprise are created, reviewed, approved, stored, retrieved, transferred, and destroyed. According to Gartner: *Records management will become a top 10 issue for many CIOs in the coming years.*

On the following pages, we will discuss the various sections of Sarbanes-Oxley that a document management solution might help with compliance:

- **Section 302:** According to Section 302, the CEO and CFO have to personally certify the financial statements and disclosures made by the company in terms of their authenticity and accuracy. This requires a system to be in place that will make the CEO and the CFO confident that all the disclosures that the company makes are accurate and authentic. This can be done in two ways:

  One is to trickle-down the responsibility of the CEO and the CFO to the lower management levels and in response bubble-up the sign-offs from the lower management levels on all documents that are input to the company filings.

  Second is to design comprehensive business processes that produce the company filings. The business processes will be designed in a very rigorous manner in order to comply with all the provisions, and proper implementation and training of all the personnel related to the business processes will be carried out and tested on a periodic basis. Further, the business processes themselves will be open to stringent internal audits that will be carried out from time to time.

A combination of both the above will go a long way towards ensuring compliance.

For both these options, it is clear that a strong, enterprise-wide document management system will provide the foundation on which the compliance will actually be carried out. In the first case, the sign-offs can be configured using a workflow module of the document management system. In the second case, the business process itself will be configured in the document management system and all the relevant supporting or input documents will be part of the DMS and appropriate subordination and linking will be done between the official company filings and all the documents input.

As proof of the records supporting the final company financials, as filed or reported, it is important to archive all the emails, spreadsheets, Instant Messages or other communications and documents that were exchanged which led to a final certified filing by the CEO and CFO. This will safeguard the CxO's claim that all the financial reports are true to their knowledge and due diligence was carried out before certifying the reports.

- **Section 404:** The CEO and CFO need to provide a report certifying that the "internal controls" have been assessed and are working fine or that there are weaknesses and appropriate action is being taken. Complying with this requirement is one of the most difficult parts of Sarbanes-Oxley and requires a whole slew of people, processes and technologies. However, DMS has an important role to play in this.

All the emails and attached documents in the chronological sequence will need to be archived for the purpose of proving that the internal controls are appropriate. Ideally, a workflow module will provide added assurance that the internal controls are implemented.

- **Section 103:** Requires storing the documents for a period of 7 years for audit companies. The company being audited should replicate the documentation to guard against any discrepancy, miscommunication or mismanagement.

- **Section 409:** Requires near-real-time reporting of all material events, whether internal or external, to the investors and the regulatory bodies. This can be accomplished by using a single, enterprise-wide document management system with appropriate "alerts," and with the notifications and workflow configured according to the design of the compliance-based business processes. This system would ensure that all relevant information is immediately relayed to top management (CEO and CFO), the compliance committee and the advisors with minimum delay or latency. DMS provides appropriate capabilities to the compliance advisors to provide a recommendation (within the stipulated time frame) linked to each alert and escalate the reports to the CxOs with the appropriate recommendations. The CxOs can then decide whether it merits disclosure under the compliance act based on recommendations of their Compliance Committee or Advisors.

- **Section 802:** Provides for criminal penalties for knowingly altering, destroying, concealing and other activities, such as introducing false records, related to impeding or influencing an ongoing or potential upcoming investigation by a federal agency. This would call for holding all documents in a secure system where absolutely no one in the company can alter them once they are finalized. Also, this calls for a formal document retention and destruction policy which is strictly adhered to (in fact, can be proven to be adhered to) and which involves ensuring that no document, which any investigating agency would require is being destroyed or deleted. Further, the act requires that as soon as the company comes to know about a potential investigation, all documents pertaining or somehow germane to that investigation are immediately ordered indestructible or unalterable by anyone, including the CxOs of the company. This makes it important to have a feature related to creating and accepting "alerts" from the legal department of the company about any ongoing or upcoming potential investigations and as a consequence, immediate information "vaulting" of all related documents. This feature will ensure compliance with this particular section and save a potential prison term and a large monetary fine, and of course, loss of credibility.

This section has a strong bearing on the records or document management policy of a company. The company must develop a suitable document management policy and adhere to it in a timely and rigorous manner. If this is not done, the company is exposed to severe costs and damage in terms of providing documents to hostile parties in "pre-trial discovery," the legal process of providing all relevant documents to the opposing party in a lawsuit. It also exposes the company to accusations of hiding or destroying relevant documents, if done at a later stage, even before any legal proceedings are begun against the company, a la Arthur Andersen's Enron-related documents.

Document Management Systems provide several benefits to the company. Since an IT system is a business process frozen in a particular software and hardware implementation, it proves that the particular business process is being consciously and diligently adhered to. In the worst case, it at least proves that the compliance is being followed in spirit. Now, whether the compliance is being followed in form can be found out from the results of the particular system and also by auditing it at various stages of the business process. The capability to follow an audit trail on all documents created or processed through it is extremely useful in executing compliance activities and also in proving compliance at a later stage. The capability to create workflows automatically creates auditable process paths. The DMS also makes it possible to access any documents at any point in time with relative ease. It also acts as a centralized repository of documents (both structured and unstructured). All publicly disclosed documents can be locked in the final form as images and cannot be tampered with later on. These can be stored and deleted according to the schedules of various regulatory and compliance Acts. Documents and information which are intended for limited consumption at the top management level, can also be strictly screened and internal controls on these can be enforced rigorously. At the appropriate time, the documents can be "published."

- **Whistleblower:** For this section of the act, it is important that a document management system is provided to log all whistleblower communication, absolutely securely, where no unauthorized personnel may be able to access it, and to store all communications.

An indirect requirement for Document Management Systems in the enterprise is for the storage of documents related to enterprise compliance policies, their updates, amendments, the internal control policies of the company and other documents of a similar nature that help in demonstrating the compliance process. The company needs to make policies about the following aspects of documents:

- Creation
- Approvals
- Publishing
- Retention
- Access
- Distribution

- Lifecycle

This policy will assist in implementing the conflicting requirements of document retention for compliance purposes and document deletion for reducing the cost of document retention and improving operational efficiency. The initial step is to define the document retention policy. The second step is to survey the existing document management systems in place in the enterprise. The third step is to create a proper document management system which adheres to the following practices:

- Have a centralized repository of documents
- Have a structured and hierarchical architecture
- Have security and access control

Security

Enterprise security is an important topic for Sarbanes-Oxley. It has implications for the overall Enterprise Technology Ecosystem security. If unauthorized access is possible on any part of the system, especially those related to or having an effect on financial data, then Sec. 302 and Sec. 404 compliance will be difficult. If the whistleblower system anonymity is threatened, then Sec. 301 compliance is compromised. Sec. 409 violations are also expected if security threatens detection of material events at the required management levels. In short, security of the Enterprise Technology Ecosystem is a fundamental issue for compliance with Sarbanes-Oxley. There are several technologies available to ensure Enterprise Security. However, it should be remembered that the "people" part is one of the weakest links in the security value chain. Hence, user training is a must. Secondly, a general principle to adhere to is: **Make human-error security violations difficult through automation and configuration of security systems.** For example:

- Deleting files unintentionally
- Sending files to unintended audience by mistake

- Gaining physical access to unauthorized systems unintentionally

Policies, procedures and processes for security are also important. There is again a recommended principle here: Don't make security procedures so complicated, difficult to adapt to, and time-consuming that people find ways to bypass them in daily operations. For example: requiring passwords to be so lengthy or difficult to remember that people tend to write them down. In the following, some of the crucial security technologies for Sarbanes-Oxley are discussed.

HIERARCHICAL ACCESS CONTROL SYSTEM

One of the excellent implementation frameworks for a hierarchical access control system is Role Based Access Control (RBAC). RBAC makes things easier and more cost effective for the enterprise to enforce security procedures.

RBAC requires that the security architecture of the technology systems be based on the organization architecture. Access is provided to particular roles in the organization based on the responsibilities they have been assigned. Access rights are restricted to the minimum resources that are required to fulfill that role and its responsibilities. Once the access rights for each role are defined, individual users are assigned more specific tasks.

This makes it easier to focus on defining the organizational architecture and operations carefully and then follow up with the RBAC definitions, instead of trying to configure each individual user's access rights. In the latter case, if the role of a particular user changes, then his or her rights need to be changed for each and every system. In RBAC, that user will be assigned a new set of roles and all the associated changes for restricting access to the systems required by the old roles and providing access to systems required by the new roles automatically get configured. So by simply changing a user's position in the organizational architecture, RBAC will allow the new access controls to be implemented.

Further, any change in the business processes or operations or organizational structure can be easily implemented by reflecting that in the RBAC, followed by attaching individuals to their new roles in the new structure and processes.

If an individual leaves the organization, removing him or her from the organization structure will close all assigned security access. The new person to join in the same role can be assigned all the access rights to the same systems by associating him or her with the appropriate location in the organization structure.

AUTHENTICATION MANAGEMENT

Authentication management means identifying the users correctly before granting access to them. How will a CFO be identified, for example? User names and passwords are the most basic means of authentication. There are other means using biometrics (fingerprint, retina scans etc.) that can be used for authentication access to the most sensitive data. There are other methods in between these two extremes such as smart cards or other hardware devices which are in possession of the appropriate individual, or digital certificates stored on particular computers, physical access to which is heavily guarded and provided only to the appropriate user.

These systems will ensure internal controls, to a large extent and in combination with proper documentation, provide proof of proper implementation of internal controls for Sec. 404.

Audit Control System

Audit control systems keep a log of all access and modification events on all the systems by:

- Other Systems
- Application Processes
- Users

They can follow and audit the trail of any event or process throughout the enterprise technology ecosystem.

158

Encryption System

These systems are useful in security at the most fundamental level of the data and document levels. These are helpful in safeguarding the data or documents, whereby even if someone gains physical access to the data, it is in an encrypted format, and can only be decrypted by the appropriate person bearing the decryption key. If the encryption algorithm is of a sufficiently large number of bits (e.g. 64 or 128 or more), then it becomes practically impossible to decrypt that information without the key.

Vulnerability Audit Systems

Periodic and ongoing audits of security vulnerability using the appropriate software systems and through manual audits carried out by qualified personnel or consultants provides yet another documentary proof of good internal controls and provides confidence on financial accuracy.

Vulnerability systems are based on a good knowledge base of known security loopholes in the Enterprise Technology Ecosystem. These are identified and marked to be addressed. Generally, there are certain specific configurations and/or other systems that can be put in place to cover the vulnerabilities.

Intrusion detection/Firewalls and Anti-Virus System

Again, this is not a direct requirement of Sarbanes-Oxley compliance, but is important for demonstrating that internal controls are in place and that they are secure and safe. It will also prevent the occurrence of data inaccuracy.

Security Policy and its Enforcement and Documentation

This will be important from the viewpoint of providing documentary proof of internal controls and will likely be the most important segment of the security infrastructure. Security technologies can be used properly only by defining a good security policy, documenting it, and enforcing it.

Training on the security policy and the security systems for the proper and maximum usage of the security systems and ongoing audits by a security committee to ensure adherence to the policy will be critical.

ISO 17799 and ISO 1335

ISO 1335: *Information technology - Guidelines for the management of IT Security.*

ISO 17799: *Information technology - Code of practice for information security management.*

Based on a Computer Security Institute and FBI joint survey, it was reported that in 30% of the companies security breaches were from internal systems, and in 77% of the companies employees were the "hackers". Auditors will consider IT as part of the internal control during an audit.[23] Hence, security breaches or vulnerability of the IT systems becomes part of the weakness in the internal control system.[24]

Security needs to be implemented throughout the "Information Value Chain." The ERP system stores data in the databases. The databases need to be secure. This data then goes into an analytics or reporting system, which is then made into a report and stored on a fileserver. All the components of the information value chain need to be secure. The interfaces between the various elements of the information value chain also need to be secure.

Finally, the reports and most of the value-added information usually rests in the form of office productivity tools, such as word processors, spreadsheets and emails exchanged between the top management and the board. These systems need to be especially secure since the likelihood of being lax are very high at this level.

---

[23] Based on Statement of Auditing Standards (SAS) #94 from the AICPA

[24] http://www.gao.gov/special.pubs/ai12.19.6.pdf provides the guidelines for auditors for internal control audits from the United States General Accounting Office.

160

Storage, Disaster Recovery and Continuity Planning

Storage is the fundamental requirement for the safekeeping of all the data and documents of the enterprise (i.e. Enterprise Information). Proper storage, its management, security and safety are important issues. Today, organizations are literally generating terabytes of data each week. Combined with requirements for storing auditor-relevant documents safely for 7 years, internal control documentations, internal audit documents etc. the storage requirement is expected to go up even further. Under these conditions, choosing the right storage technology and architecture is important.

Hardware technologies like RAID (Redundant Array of Inexpensive Disks) are much better than JBODs (Just a Bunch of Disks) since RAID provides some fault tolerance at the disk level itself. The architecture to use these in, such as a NAS or a SAN, is still a very difficult question. But it is expected that most organizations will have several NAS servers in place soon. If the enterprise is very large and is looking at a long-term solution for its storage, then SAN architecture might be the way to go. The NAS devices, in which investment has already been made, can be integrated into the SAN architecture.

Both these architectures are designed to ease the pressure on the network as well as centralize the Enterprise Information. While NAS is a good solution at the workgroup or department level, SAN is the solution for the long-term enterprise level storage requirements.

Again, there is no direct requirement in Sarbanes-Oxley to install SAN or NAS, but the acquisition of these will be essential since the information storage requirements dictated by Sarbanes-Oxley sections definitely require large amounts of storage. Further, the requirements of internal controls and real-time notification of material events dictate storage systems from which data can be retrieved and processed efficiently.

Disaster Recovery is an important requirement to prove that all documents are retained and available to the investigating agencies and hence safeguards the organization from Sec. 802 violations. Further, this shows that several potential material events are already taken care of. Also, all documents will be safe for the required 7-year period and for any agency investigations that might need them.

Business Continuity Planning will be more important from an operational viewpoint rather than from a Sarbanes-Oxley requirements perspective. Nevertheless, it makes good business sense to have it in place.

COMMUNICATION AND NETWORKING

A good communication and networking system is important for providing a solid communications infrastructure between the operational and executive management to supply information in real-time about material events. Further, an anonymous and secure communication system is required by the Whistleblower requirement of Sec. 301.

The Internal Controls requirement of Sec. 404 and the financial accuracy requirements of Sec. 302 also require a secure communication system, since a lot of important command and controls are implemented through email and messaging systems and important financial information travels through these communication channels.

Enterprise Integration: Data Integrity and Multiple Systems

For Sarbanes-Oxley compliance, the sections on reporting "significant events" and also accurate and timely financial and other data show that there is a need for bringing all the data together. The need to have auditable internal controls also requires that all the data is integrated and works across various business processes and is traceable. Sections 302, 404 and 409 call for a massive enterprise integration effort.

Financial accuracy demands a highly integrated enterprise. If the information from the trio of core transactional systems (ERP, SCM, CRM) and other supporting functional automation systems is not integrated, the financial data will remain inaccurate and large amounts of resources will be required to reconcile the differing, though overlapping, data from the various sources.

162

This data then remains open to distortion, data loss and corruption. Further, it becomes easy to prove the inadequacy of internal controls. All the places where the data comes out of the transaction systems and is then entered into the financial reporting systems is a point of vulnerability due to unintentional human errors and intentional mischief. The possibility of providing real-time reports of material events under Sec. 409 is extremely difficult with a non-integrated enterprise.

There are several integration technologies available today and the CIO will have to choose the appropriate one based on the specific requirements and constraints of the organization. The main technologies are:

- Enterprise Application Integration
- Web Services
- Middleware
- Business Process Integration and
- Data integration[25]

It is challenging to choose the right technology from this array. In fact, chances are that all of these technologies already exist in the organization and that compounds the problem.

EAI is a reliable technology and web services (or more generally Service-Oriented Architectures) are the integration tools of the future. Hence, a combination of both these technologies will need to be adopted.

Once all the data from any application is converted into XML, it becomes much easier to make it accessible and available to any other applications. These applications can then use this data to provide whatever reports are required for regulatory purposes.

EAI legacy tools that are available in the organization, combined with Service Oriented Architecture based on web services and XML-based data storage, are

---

[25] There are several more with slight differentiations and it becomes difficult to differentiate the offerings except by chronology and the original platform design time (i.e. when it was first introduced).

recommended for enabling Sarbanes-Oxley compliance and better business practices.

Current Enterprise Technology Ecosystem: What does it deliver?

It is important to first audit the capabilities of the existing or current technology ecosystem. The audit has to be done from the perspective of compliance with Sarbanes-Oxley. A few CIOs might realize that they are already close to compliance. They just need to gain a clear understanding of what the Sarbanes-Oxley rules require and then configure a few functions in the key technology systems to achieve compliance.

Most CIOs will need to perform a detailed study from the ecosystem perspective. The overall system will have to be evaluated for compliance. If the overall system seems healthy and can cope with compliance, and ideally this would be the typical case, then the next step will be to identify parts of the system that could potentially lead to noncompliance. Most of the effort for compliance should be focused on these parts. What is wrong with these parts or species or components? Can they be reconfigured to manage compliance? Can they be supported by some manual systems to achieve compliance? Can these systems be supported by some new utilities? Is a fundamental redesign of the business process called for? Or should a new IT system be brought in to replace these parts?

Is your IT Infrastructure Sarbanes-Oxley Compliant?

Do a self-evaluation using the following checklist:

Questions	Remarks
Do your transactional systems share data between them?	
How many major transactional systems (ERP, SCM, CRM etc.) exist in your organization?	
Are all of these on a single database platform? If yes, then is it the same version?	
If no, then are they integrated with each other?	
Are all of these on the same or similar	

164

operating system platform? If yes, then is it the same version?	
What other minor transactional systems exist in the organization?	
What legacy systems are being used in the organization?[26]	
What reporting systems are being used in the organization?	
What analysis tools exist?	
What business intelligence or knowledge management tools exist?	
Can an unauthorized person or software or IT user or any other entity gain access to the financial information of the company?	
Is there possibility of data loss?	
Is the organization's IT infrastructure dependent on few important people? Or is it more process driven? What happens if these people leave their jobs, get sick or for some reason are not available to the enterprise for an extended period? Will the IT function keep working reasonably well with the help of other staff?	
Are documents stored properly? Can they be retrieved on demand? Can these documents be stored for the long-term (at least 7 years)? Are they safe from risks of fire, floods, earthquakes, terrorist attacks and other higher or lower forms of risk to their existence?	
How close to real-time is the information delivery at the organization? Can material events or operational risks be detected and reported as early as two days from the occurrence?	
Can you "certify" that your financial reporting is accurate?	
Can you "certify" that the internal controls	

---

[26] *"Legacy Software is critical software that cannot be modified efficiently."—Source: http://www.dur.ac.uk/CSM/SABA/legacy-wksp1/meaning.doc*

are in place to prevent intentional or unintentional distortion to financial data?	

The above checklist provides a feel for the kind of IT infrastructure it will take to achieve Sarbanes-Oxley compliance. It might seem that "throwing" a whole lot of technology at it can provide Sarbanes-Oxley compliance. However, nothing could be further from truth. It is the stated position in this book that:

"80% of the companies have 80% of the technology required to achieve Sarbanes-Oxley compliance."

What is required is not more technology per se, rather the effective use of the existing technology with the goal of aligning it with the requirements of Sarbanes-Oxley. In general, the existing technology might need to be supplemented by minor technology buys.

CHAPTER 15
THE PROCESS

INTRODUCTION TO THE PROCESS

One of the key ingredients for the success of a Sarbanes-Oxley compliance effort is "process." Process gives us a step-by-step, structured approach to the "implementation".

SOCKET Vision

• **Immediate:** Foolproof implementation of Sarbanes-Oxley Compliant Key Enterprise Technologies across the organization; any change in the SOCKET Ecosystem should be arrived at via a structured approach without affecting the Sarbanes-Oxley compliance of the system.
• **Long-term:** Achieve strategic enterprise goals through proper encapsulation of key business processes in the SOCKET Ecosystem.

SOCKET Strategy

To address Sarbanes-Oxley compliance across the organization, the SOCKET strategy has to be carefully created keeping in mind that *"80% of the companies already have 80% of the technology they need in order to achieve Sarbanes-Oxley compliance."* This is best done by leveraging the existing body of knowledge on Sarbanes-Oxley from consultancies, publications and other learning channels. More focus should be given to long-term strategy rather than short-term or corrective approaches. Further, compliance with Sarbanes-Oxley makes good business sense, since the requirements dictate following business practices that lead to an efficient and self-aware organization.

Team Definition

A full-time, dedicated team is required for the success of a Sarbanes-Oxley compliance project. Roles, responsibilities, authority and deliverables should be clearly defined.

Appointment of a CCO and a SOCC

A top executive, namely a CCO (Chief Compliance Officer)[27] with "clout" in the Management Council and the Board of Directors will lead the team. This executive (let us call him/her "The Sarbanes-Oxley Champion") is the overall in-charge of Sarbanes-Oxley implementation across the organization. S/he reports directly to the CEO and takes help and guidance from the CFO and the finance team.

The "Sarbanes-Oxley Champion" has a "high-powered" Sarbanes-Oxley Compliance Committee (SOCC), which includes the COO, location heads, corporate heads etc. A high-level team of senior Sarbanes-Oxley consultants[28] assists the SOCC. The Sarbanes-Oxley consulting (external) team consists of Technology Consultants, Business Process Consultants, Risk Management Consultants, Internal Controls Consultants, Legal Consultants, and Sarbanes-Oxley Audit Specialists.

The CIO (Chief Information Officer), who is also the SOCKET Head, supports the "Sarbanes-Oxley Champion" or CCO. The COO (or VP-Operations or

---

[27] The CCO will usually be a person with a legal and financial background and who has an understanding of the enterprise functioning at the broad or big-picture level and also at the detailed level. S/he should have the appropriate authority within the company and the CEO, CFO and CIO should be accessible to him/her. The key personnel in the enterprise should also believe in his/her capability and expertise. The person can be either a consultant or a home-grown officer with a long history in that organization.

[28] Preferably *external* Sarbanes-Oxley specialist consultants so that the objectivity and authority is maintained.

168

equivalent), who understands middle management and has enough clout at the operational level, supports the CIO. They are supported by the Corporate IT Head (VP-IT operations or the IT manager who reports to the CIO).

The Corporate IT head works with a highly-qualified team consisting of experts in Functional/Business Analysis, Technology, Applications, Information, Hardware, Networking etc. They are supported by a dedicated IT development team and consultants, and hardware, networking, and database experts working at various locations and managing the IT infrastructure. The Corporate IT Head is supported at different locations by an IT Location[29] head; we will refer to him/her as SLC (SOCKET Location Coordinator). The Corporate IT head is supported by SLC1, SLC2, and SLC3 ... etc. depending on number of locations. Each SLC is supported by SSLCs (SOCKET Sub-Location[30] Coordinators) who are the part of the location and who actively support the business. The SOCKET team consists of n Audit Team and an Implementation Team. Each team has distinct roles and they work in collaboration for the success of SOCKET.

SOCKET Audit Team

The SOCKET Audit team consists of experts who understand the domain of IT and who have a thorough understanding of business operations, functional knowledge, business process, and financial and legal regulations. The team consists of professionals who have worked in functional areas and handled the key business processes. The main function of this group is to conduct audits of all key business processes and of the enterprise technology ecosystem across the organization, and after the implementation to conduct audits of all the work done by the SOCKET implementation team. Post-implementation, this team has the responsibility to conduct Internal Audits at regular intervals and obtain feedback at the operational levels. They are responsible for closing all NCRs (Non-

---

[29] Location refers to the geographic location of a business unit.
[30] Sub-location refers to specific departments or workgroups within each Location or Business Unit.

compliance Reports) and oversee that the gap analysis, risk control plan and internal control projects are delivering as per the requirements. This team has the SLC overseeing and the SSLC conducting the internal audits at all locations. The team works closely with the Sarbanes-Oxley Compliance Committee and SOCKET implementation team.

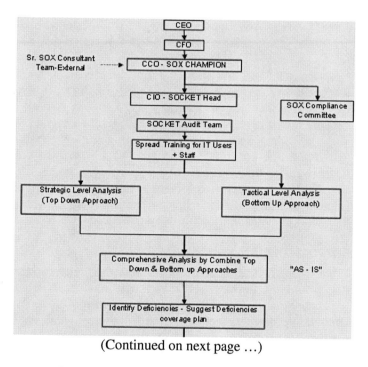

(Continued on next page ...)

SOCKET Implementation Team

The SOCKET implementation team consists of experts in IT: System and Architecture Analysis, Databases, Enterprise and Transactions Applications, Integration Tools, Software Development, Hardware, Networking, amongst others. Their main function is to provide IT solutions, that is, to develop, configure, align, integrate, and customize business process and customized requirements for Sarbanes-Oxley compliance. They are

170

supported at different locations by an IT location head referred to as the SLC[31] (SOCKET Location Coordinator). The Corporate IT head is supported by SLC1, SLC2, SLC3 … etc. depending on the number of locations. Each SLC is supported by SSLCs (SOCKET Sub-Location[32] Coordinators) who are the part of the location and are actively supporting the business.

(… Continued from previous page)

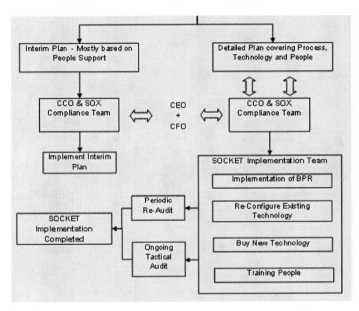

(Downloadable at www.SarbanesOxleyGuide.com)

External Consulting Team

The CIO and SOCKET heads work closely with 3-5 (depending on the requirement and the size of the organization) external Sarbanes-Oxley consultants per

---

[31] Note that the SLC and SSLC of the implementation team are different from the SLC and SSLC of the Audit team to avoid role conflict.

[32] Sub-location refers to specific departments or workgroups within each Location or Business Unit.

location who are experts in Information Technology, Business Process Integration, Risk Control Analysis, Internal Controls and Sarbanes-Oxley Audits.

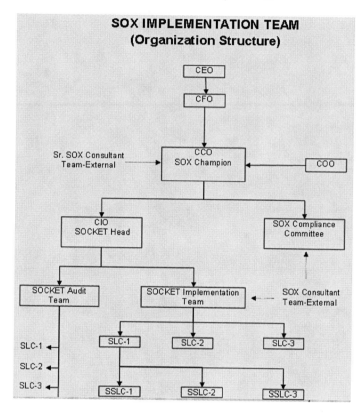

Awareness and Training

Before initiating Sarbanes-Oxley compliance, all the team members should undergo detailed and extensive "learning" (that is, an advanced level of understanding beyond mere training) on Sarbanes-Oxley. All top and mid-level management should undergo training and workshops on Sarbanes-Oxley.

"As-Is" Analysis

After this, the organization should undergo an "As-Is" Analysis Audit, carried out by the SOCKET Audit Team, which will help in benchmarking against each

172

section and area for Sarbanes-Oxley Compliance. The company can use the help of external consultants to assist the SOCKET Audit Team for this. The objective is to get a clear picture of the status of the organization vis-à-vis Sarbanes-Oxley compliance.

STRATEGIC (TOP-DOWN) APPROACH

Strategic Level Analysis looks at the overall aspects of the organization. It takes a "from the top down" approach for identification of gaps and shortcomings in the overall SOCKET ecosystem.

SOCKET Ecosystem Audit

A preliminary study needs to be carried out on the entire organization. Here are the steps:

1. List the key Business Processes (BP) of the Company:
   i. BP1
   ii. BP2
   iii. BP3
   iv. Etc.

2. For each Business Process, make a list of the software applications (APP) that are utilized to automate the whole or a part of the Business Process:
   i. APP1
   ii. APP2
   iii. APP3
   iv. Etc.

3. For each Software Application, make a list of the Sub-Business Processes (SBP) it automates:
   i. SBP1
   ii. SBP2
   iii. SBP3
   iv. Etc.

4. Then scan the list of SBPs and put the SBPs in a sequence that recreates the complete automated Key Business Process.

5. Mark out the applications that span more than one Key Business Processes.

6. With this in place, start checking the SBP sequence to see how information is transferred across the interface from one Application (automating a particular SBP) to another (automating the successive SBP).

7. Verify and validate the data that gets transferred across each interface. Does what enters the information creation point of the Business Process remain consistent with what comes out? Is there data loss during the travel of information across the SBP application sequence?

8. Most importantly: Are all financial data accurate, consistent and validated?

9. Are adequate internal controls in place across all the applications and interfaces?

Following the above study, a more specific and detailed study needs to be carried out. Extensive study of the entire organization is done with the help of internal and external audit teams. Audits are conducted in following areas:

Business Process Audit

- Identify and list the key business processes.
- Break down each Business Process (BP) into sub-processes.
- How do various BP relate to each other?
- Benchmark your business processes against industry standards.
- Is there a plan for adapting Business Processes, IT etc. of potential acquired or merged companies after acquisition or merger?
- Determine localization and linguistic issues.

174

Information Audit

- Map the "Information Value Chain".
- Identify points of information creation (for example: order taking, payment or purchase).
- Is the appropriate information captured at the point of creation? What is the method used to capture this information? Have the appropriate forms been designed? Information might come in different media: paper forms, emails, websites, databases, fax, phone etc.
- Storing and Archiving of information
- Retrieval and Display of information
- Information Distribution
- Analysis, Reporting and Visualization
- Inferences and Decisions

Application Audit

- List all software applications.
- Identify points of information creation for each application, that is, all input forms for each application. Do these forms allow the capture of relevant information as per the information audit?
- What is the method used to capture information from different media (hand-filled or printed forms, emails, faxes, web-based forms etc.)?
- Is all the data being captured through the applications? Are all the fields in the forms mapped to the fields in the applications? Are all the fields in the form being captured? Are there missing fields either in the application or in the form?
- What are the databases used for storing various pieces of information?
- What is the sequence of applications automating the information value chain for each business process?
- Can the data be transferred from one application to the next? Is this via a common database or

interlinking software or other integration mechanisms, or is it done through spreadsheet files or manual re-keying?

- Data Validation: Is the data being generated at the creation point and is the data arriving after traveling through the sequence of applications the same?
- Can the data be stored and retrieved easily?
- Which is the "Master ERP", or the master application for each business process?
- Is there a master application for all Business Processes? Does it provide reports to the CEO/CFO? Is this real-time and if not, how delayed?

Technology Audit

- List the technology elements supporting these processes and sub-processes.
- Identify and list the software applications supporting these processes.
- List the hardware systems supporting these processes.
- List the networking systems.
- List the databases.
- Assess:
  - Speed
  - Architecture
  - Storage capacity
  - Performance
  - Scalability
  - Backup
  - DR (redundancy, failover)
  - BCP (Business Continuity Planning)
  - Web-enablement
- Identify legacy systems.
- Are there systems or parts that might fail eventually?
- Are there systems or parts no longer supported by the manufacturer/supplier?

176

- Is there an IT vision document? Does it align with the strategic vision?
- Is the existing IT infrastructure aligned with the IT vision?
- Change Management Processes: If a new application or technology is introduced or an old one is retired or any modification takes place, is there a mechanism to notify the appropriate authorities about it and evaluate the impact on Sarbanes-Oxley?
- Are there systems to alert the IT heads if any unauthorized software or technology is introduced?
- Are there identification techniques for applications and technology?
- Is there a proper inventory of the IT systems?
- Is there a phase-out mechanism for the IT systems?
- Are the TCO and ROI of all the major systems tracked and benchmarked with the industry standards and against the promised TCO and ROI at the purchase/acquisition time?

A key question the Audit Committee asks during the above audit pertains to data integrity, and hence, financial data accuracy and internal controls. Also relevant is the speed of information travel across the enterprise through various applications and systems, and related information security issues. Detailed documentation of the Strategic Level Analysis is made and submitted to the CIO-SOCKET Head. This document will cover the status, action plan, recommendations etc.

TACTICAL (BOTTOM-UP) APPROACH

Tactical Level Analysis looks into operational aspects across the organizations. It takes a bottom-up approach for identification of gaps and shortcomings in the overall SOCKET Ecosystem. With the Tactical Approach, we uncover gaps which are more operational in nature from the user's point of view. For this, a NCR (Non Compliance Report) form is designed to assist in capturing the Tactical or Operational "Gap" (see NCR form below). This is also called a problem-solving form. This form helps in documenting and understanding the problem or noncompliance area and helps in formulating a PDCA (Plan-Do-Check-Act) analysis for problem solving and achieving compliance.

Any employee who feels that the systems are not working as per requirements can submit a report to the Tactical Audit team and fill out a NCR form. To encourage employees to fill and analyze the "Gap" a suitable reward or incentive may be created. This can accelerate the audit and implementation process and the awareness of Sarbanes-Oxley across the organization. A detailed document is prepared at the end of the Tactical Audit and findings, suggestions, and an action plan submitted.

SOCKET Non-Compliance Report (NCR)

SOCKET :	Date :	NCR No.:

SOCKET Avenues	H/w Sys. S/w App.S/w N/w Database People Process

SOCKET Location:	Sub Location:	SLC:	SSLC:

Step1:Define Non-Compliance	Step2: Observation
SECTION:	
	Step 3: Analysis
	Step 4: Plan
Name & Sign of Auditee : Internal Auditor :	

Objective Measure for	
Desired situation	
Actual situation	*Don't forget to implement and verify the effectiveness of interim (containment) corrections*

Step 5: What Action Taken? Role played?	By Whom?	Step 6: Result Achieved & verified?

Step 7: Next Action	NCR Evaluation
	Proactive Action: 1
	Root-cause eliminated: 1
	Near-nil investment made: 1

Business Process Document Update:	NC closing date: Sign of Auditor :
	Sign of CCO:
Remarks:	

(Form is downloadable at www.SarbanesOxleyGuide.com)

MONITORING THE AUDIT TEAM

The SOCKET Audit team will be monitored by the Sarbanes-Oxley Compliance Committee at the corporate level. After the training phase and on a periodic and ongoing basis, the Sarbanes-Oxley compliance committee will conduct audits throughout the organization to ensure that the SOCKET audit team is carrying out its mandate in a systematic and thorough manner. The Sarbanes-Oxley Compliance Committee may develop a checklist for conducting the audit based on the one given below.

Checklist for Monitoring the SOCKET Audit Team By the Sarbanes-Oxley Compliance Committee and Audit of Socket Location Coordinators

Seq. No.	Point to be audited	Remarks of the Auditor
1	Is there sufficient evidence that all the "auditees" have gone through the SOCKET Guidebook?	
2	Is there sufficient evidence that all the "auditees" have gone through and understood the major Sections and Implications of Sarbanes-Oxley?	
3	Is there sufficient evidence that all the "auditees" have gone through and understood the roles of CEO, CFO, CIO, CCO and Sarbanes-Oxley Audit and Implementation Team?	
4	Is there sufficient and documentary evidence that the IT team has given regular reports on any major changes or additions in the systems, which might have an impact	

Seq. No.	Point to be audited	Remarks of the Auditor
	on Sarbanes-Oxley compliance?	
5	Is there sufficient and documentary evidence that all the "auditees" have conducted the compliance meetings regularly with the IT and users staff?	
6	Is there sufficient and documentary evidence that the "auditees" have invited the top-level Sarbanes-Oxley compliance committee for the periodic SOCKET presentations?	
7	Is there documentary evidence to prove that the Compliance Meetings have been recorded and progress tracked by the SOCKET team?	
8	Is there sufficient and documentary evidence that the SOCKET team has identified, imparted and maintained the records of SOCKET training?	
9	Is there sufficient evidence that the SOCKET Location Coordinators have analyzed the periodic compliance reports about any new IT system or changes to the existing systems?	
10	Is there evidence that there is an analysis done of reported SOCKET Non-Compliance Reports (NCR) that have come through IT staff/users?	

Seq. No.	Point to be audited	Remarks of the Auditor
11	Is there an analysis done by the SOCKET Location Coordinators that the implementation of SOCKET has resulted in the cultural and attitudinal change in the organization?	

Comprehensive Analysis

The CIO will go through the Strategic Level Analysis and Tactical Level Analysis documents. A comprehensive detailed report will be jointly prepared, which will give a clear picture of the organization status. Based on this, and with the help of Sarbanes-Oxley consultants, a "Gap Analysis" is done with respect to Sarbanes-Oxley compliance. Also, Risk Control areas and Internal Control systems need to be identified at this stage. Two reports will be prepared:

Interim Compliance Plan

This report will be corrective in nature and will focus on the immediate steps to be taken for controlling the risk and temporary arrangements for Sarbanes-Oxley compliance. This will involve mostly solutions related to the allocation of manpower (or people) support.

This report will be submitted to the CCO or Sarbanes-Oxley Champion. S/he will analyze the report findings and suggested project plan with the help of Sarbanes-Oxley consultants and the Sarbanes-Oxley Compliance team. After finalizing the Interim Compliance Plan, the final "go-ahead" will be given by CEO and CFO.